TABLE OF CONTENTS

CHAPTER 15

THE IMPORTANCE OF MARKETING – HOW MARKETING IS EVERYTHING **151**

CHAPTER 16

IMPORTANCE OF CREATING A UNIQUE COMPETITIVE ADVANTAGE (UNIQUE SELLING PROPOSITION) **169**

CHAPTER 17

ELEVATING YOUR SELF-CONCEPT AND ITS IMPACT ON SELF-ESTEEM AND SELF-WORTH **181**

CONCLUSION

CHAPTER 1

A NEW BEGINNING IN REGENERATIVE MEDICINE IS UPON US. HOW WILL YOU TAKE ADVANTAGE OF IT?

How Big Is The Anti-Aging Trend?

Anti-aging is termed as the techni□ue designed to prevent the appearance of getting older. Anti-aging refers to the process of limiting or retarding these changes through various products and services. Nowadays, good physical personality has become a necessity and determines the success of an individual in different areas of life. The growing consciousness among both the young and old consumers regarding their physical appearance has fostered the demand for anti-aging products and devices.

Over the past few generations, perceptions, attitudes, and behaviors related to aging have changed. While past generations adopted a more passive, less involved view of aging, now people are taking a very active, complex, and deliberate approach to anti-aging.

Aging is achieved by a series of diverse biochemical procedures in the body that persuade it, both internally and externally. These biochemical procedures cause the body to deteriorate over a timeframe, affecting the wellbeing, wellness and physical appearance of an aging person. Anti-aging involves procedures and medication intentional to delay, stop or retard the aging process. Recently, there has been a significant increase in the anti-aging phenomenon.

The desire to retain a younger look and feel isn't restricted to an older generation. Modern men and women are making changes in their lifestyles

In the beginning there is the stem cell; it is the origin of an organism's life.

~ Stewart Sell

to increase their life spans. They are beginning their skin care treatments at a younger age and are spending more time and money on products that minimize the signs of aging. With younger consumers hoping to preserve their youth before the onset of aging, the consumer group for anti-aging products expands from middle-aged and older consumers to younger consumers between 26 to 38 years.

The trend in aging solutions, like cosmetic surgery, is also changing. People are shifting from difficult reconstructive procedures to delicate, less invasive options. On the basis of services, the anti-aging market is divided into anti-pigmentation therapy, anti-adult acne therapy, breast augmentation, liposuction, chemical peel, hair restoration treatment, others.

How Much Money Is Spent On Anti-Aging In 2017 And What Is The Expected Amount Spent In 10 Years?

Over the past two decades, declining fertility and mortality rates have resulted in a rise in the aging population, globally. The strong desire among men and women to retain youthful appearances has groomed and nurtured the cosmetics industry, worldwide. Rapidly aging demographics has led to a robust demand for anti-aging products in order to prevent wrinkles, age spots, dry skin, uneven skin tone, and even hair damages, creating room for innovations in cosmetics, thus boosting the industry growth.

Global anti-aging market size is currently in a highly growing or in a developmental stage; and as such, led by experimental studies and customer reception. One of the market restraints is the skepticism portrayed by consumers toward the global anti-aging market's services and products. One of the factors that could resolve this is the proven advancement in technologies that help create better services and products.

The global anti-aging market has reached a value of nearly US$ 47 Billion in 2017. The market is further projected to reach a value of nearly US$ 74 Billion by 2023, at a CAGR of 8% during 2018-2023. Aging is brought

We aren't made of drugs, we're made of cells. Stem cells, or stem cells in combination with pharmaceuticals, will be the future of medicine.

~ Cade Hildreth

about by a cycle of biochemical processes which cause the body to degenerate over a period of time, impacting the health, fitness and physical appearance of the individual. The future of the anti-aging market looks good with opportunities in skin care and hair care. The global anti-aging market is expected to reach an estimated $66.2 billion by 2023 with a CAGR of 5.7% from 2018 to 2023. The major growth drivers for this market are the growing aging population and increasing awareness about the advantages of using anti-aging products.

Lastly, by 2050, the population over 60 years of age is expected to reach 2.09 billion. The life expectancy for women is predicted to rise from 82.8 years in 2005 to 86.3 years in 2050. Whereas for men, the expected increase for men in the corresponding period is from 78.4 to 83.6 years. Notably, the share of older adults for cosmetic products is on the rise.

Why Is Anti-Aging So Big?

The anti-aging market is observed to be one of the rising markets in today's world. New technologies have initiated the association of new anti-aging treatments and products, which is propelling the anti-aging products, service, and devices market growth. Increased awareness about aging signs, increase in obesity, and a sedentary routine is fuelling the market growth.

Increasing aging population worldwide is another major driving factor for the anti-aging market. Strict regulations have led to the introduction of safe and efficient anti-aging products and services in the market expected to drive the anti-aging market in the near future. Furthermore, increasing consumer demand for anti-aging products and technical advancement in anti-aging services are the factors that drive the growth of the anti-aging market. However, consumers are still doubtful about some of the anti-aging services and products this factor can hamper the market growth in the future.

This field [stem cell research] isn't growing, it's exploding.

~ Barth Green

Also, the growing aging population worldwide, an increasing number of medical tourism for cosmetic procedures, rising consumer demand for anti-aging products, and the strict regulations are the other factors driving the market. Moreover, these factors have led to the introduction of safe and efficient anti-aging products and services in the market.

How Is Stem Cell Different Than Traditional Anti-Aging Therapies?

Stem cells are the building blocks of the entire body. They form the foundation of our body's repair and regeneration system, and actually, predate every other type of cell during birth. Before brain cells, heart cells, or lung tissue cells develop, stem cells are present. Stem cells are incredibly versatile, capable of changing themselves into almost any other type of cell in the body to help repair and regenerate damaged areas. They can rebuild bone, tendon tissue, muscle tissue, lung and organ tissue, and more.

These cells have also been linked to the aging process. That is, as our bodies age, the number of stem cells within them decreases. While stem cells can renew themselves, they do eventually die.

Ultimately, the fight against visible signs of aging continues. The use of allogeneic stem cells is a promising development, though, which may have a significant positive impact over time. With the use of youthful, high-energy allogenic stem cells, it may be possible to slow and even temporarily halt the aging process, although greater research is needed in this area.

Stem cell therapies are the ultimate anti-aging treatment. They are uni☐ue because they use a patient's stem cells and can be transplanted where they are needed. Treatments replenish the body with a fresh supply of concentrated stem cells to allow the repair and rejuvenation process in all organs, including skin. This is where the most obvious effects can be seen.

If power is defined as the ability to do anything and create anything, then the stem cell is the most powerful *known* life force.

~ Anonymous

Unlike plastic surgery that addresses surface looks alone and not the cause; stem cells replace, regrow, repair and rejuvenate on a cellular level that goes far beyond appearances. They restore more youthful levels of energy and resolve age-related damage to face, body, and organs. Unlike cosmetic treatments, stem cells are not a temporary solution. Unlike injectables, stem cells do not rely on using a potential toxin to alleviate the signs of aging. Unlike cosmetic surgery, there is no recovery time with stem cell treatments.

Anti-aging therapy improves the overall health, strength, and function of organs and cells, making them younger, stronger, and robust. They allow you to be more active and feel youthful again. There are two types of stem cells used for combating the signs of aging – autologous stem cells and allogeneic stem cells. Autologous stem cells are the better known, but least effective. These are your own body's stem cells harvested from fat tissue, usually. They are less effective because, well, they're as old as your body. They're not particularly energetic. They have accumulated a lot of damage and many mutations, as well.

What Is The Bold Promise Of Stem Cell Therapy?

There are several types of conditions that are either currently being treated with stem cell-based therapies or that hold out the prospect for such therapies in the future. These include autoimmune diseases, neurological disorders, cancers, and infertility. Furthermore, stem cells may be used in regenerative medicine to replace or repair tissues and organs damaged by disease or injury.

Many stem cell therapies are based on the regenerative capacities of stem cells to produce a variety of tissues, either in the patient's body or in vitro. Other therapies rely on transplanted stem cells, particularly adult mesenchymal stem cells (a type of multipotent stem cell), to provide signals that modify or regulate the activities of nearby cells without actually integrating into the patient's tissues. At present, treatments in regular

The regenerative medicine revolution is upon us. Like iron and steel to the industrial revolution, like the microchip to the tech revolution, stem cells will be the driving force of this next revolution.

~ Cade Hildreth

clinical use are limited to adult stem cells, although clinical trials have begun for deriving induced pluripotent stem (iPS) cells from patients to help researchers study diseases and the U.S.

Additionally, doctors have recently used hematopoietic stem cells to successfully culture human red blood cells in vitro, which they used in blood transfusions. The cultured red blood cells were able to survive and mature into fully functioning cells in the patients' bloodstreams, demonstrating the potential of these cells to serve as an alternative to conventional blood donation.

In order to cultivate these cells in vitro, researchers needed to find the right mix of growth factors that would coax the hematopoietic stem cells to differentiate successfully. While this represents a breakthrough in stem cell therapy that will surely be beneficial to many patients in need of blood transfusions, the fact that we have only recently been able to use stem cells to regenerate red blood cells is indicative of the challenges facing the development of in vitro tissue and organ regeneration.

What Is Possible With Stem Cell Therapy When It Comes To Regeneration?

Anyone who has owned a car or a house knows that unless you constantly maintain it and conduct repairs, it is not going to last very long. That's true for our bodies as well. In fact, there is evidence to suggest that within many of our tissues and organs live a relatively small number of adult stem cells that can repair or replace tissues and parts of organs damaged by injury or disease. These cells, which may represent sentries remaining from our embryonic development, also play an essential role in what is termed "homeostatic maintenance" – keeping our organs in a constant state of health through renewal.

Regenerative medicine, the most recent and emerging branch of medical science, deals with the functional restoration of tissues or organs for the

Stem cell research can revolutionize medicine, more than anything since antibiotics.

~ Ronald Reagan

patient suffering from severe injuries or chronic disease. The spectacular progress in the field of stem cell research has laid the foundation for cell-based therapies of disease which cannot be cured by conventional medicines. The indefinite self-renewal and potential to differentiate into other types of cells represent stem cells as frontiers of regenerative medicine. The transdifferentiating potential of stem cells varies with source and according to that regenerative applications also change.

Stem cell therapies capable of regenerating any human tissue damaged by injury, disease or aging. The repair system, similar to the method used by salamanders to regenerate limbs, could be used to repair everything from spinal discs to bone fractures and has the potential to transform current treatment approaches to regenerative medicine.

There are different types of stem cells including embryonic stem (ES) cells, which during embryonic development generate every type of cell in the human body, and adult stem cells, which are tissue-specific. There are no adult stem cells that regenerate multiple tissue types.

How Can You As A Chiropractor Take Advantage Of This Amazing Trend?

Today, stem cell therapy is one of the most innovative and effective ways to help our patients heal and possibly avoid surgery. Stem cell technology has made headlines for years, but do you actually know what these tiny cells are? Quite simply, stem cells are the earliest versions of the different cells that make up your body. Because they have the potential to become tissue, bone, hair, skin, and more, stem cells are often called the building blocks of the human body. As stem cells divide, they replenish different parts of the body by generating specialized cells to replace and regenerate injured parts.

Major surgeries such as back surgeries or joint replacements come with serious risks, limited success rates, and slow and painful recovery times.

The next age of medicine will revolve around stem cells. Just like there was the 'pre internet' age, there will soon be the 'pre stem cell age' and it will confuse the next generation to talk about it.

~ Anonymous

You might be fighting surgery, suffering from chronic pain, degenerative issues, or even sports injuries and feel you don't have another option. It may not seem that there are many alternatives, but we offer natural treatments such as stem cell regenerative therapy, which is available without the risks of surgery and long, difficult recovery periods.

Stem cell therapy can repair damaged tissue in the body as a result of disease, age, and degeneration. These treatments can potentially pinpoint damaged areas, remove swelling with powerful anti-inflammatory properties, and possibly heal these areas by regenerating new tissue and cells.

Patients that use stem cell therapy can potentially experience not only a decrease in pain but also an improvement in range of motion within weeks. The results patients have experienced are unbelievable, with many patients finding they only need one treatment!

Stem cell injections, for instance, offer the ability to heal damaged tissue naturally. With stem cell therapy, stem cells from tissues are injected directly into the affected area of the body. These stem cells have strong anti-inflammatory properties. However, stem cell therapy goes far beyond the benefits of standard "injection therapy."

Why Is It That Chiropractic And Stem Cell Therapy Are Synergistic?

Chiropractors believe in the power of the body to heal, but what we forget is that as we get older, the bandwith by which the body can heal itself as intelligently as possible becomes compromised because of this thing called aging. So do Chiropractors help unleah Innate Intelligence? Yes, but Innate becomes not so intelligent as we get older. The promise of stem cells is that we can restore the full power of the Innate intelligence and its bandwith of healing. Chiropractic and Stem Cell therapy is a marriage made in heaven. What's interesting is that medical doctors have had access to this type of

Stem cells are located throughout our bodies, like a reserve army offering regeneration and repair.

~ Samantha Bresnahan

regenerative therapy for years, and yet they have been sitting on it for all of this time because it doesn't really fit their model. Chiropractic care is designed to harness your body's own ability to heal. Today, stem cell therapy is one of the most innovative and effective ways to help our patients heal and possibly avoid surgery. There are two general categories of medical applications for stem cells: first, as an actual therapy, and second, as a way to model diseases to help researchers develop treatments.

Like the chiropractic care, stem cells are the next frontier of medicine, used to treat osteoarthritis, back pain, and all sorts of chronic diseases. Mesenchymal stem cells are found in the bone marrow cavity, the peripheral blood, and adipose tissue.

What Does The Future Of Health Care Look Like With Stem Cell Therapy And Regenerative Medicine?

Regenerative medicine is based on regenerating damaged human tissue and organs. Debilitating and terminal health conditions would not only be treatable with regenerative medicine but be made reversible. The era of regenerative medicine is upon us. Rapidly advancing medical knowledge is leading to the development of powerful new gene-based therapies that will transform medical practice, allowing most people to live much longer and healthier lives. Unlike most medicines today, regenerative medicines use human cells and substances to regrow tissue.

Regenerative medicine is an exciting endeavor at this point in history, and it attracts a range of individuals in many careers. Many university organizations now have student groups which aim to educate the community on the potential of regenerative medicine and to inspire a generation of innovators who may change the way we think of disease and recovery. These organizations are providing young adults the opportunity to network with researchers in regenerative medicine, where they can learn first-hand the opportunities in the field.

In the beginning there is the stem cell; it is the origin of an organism's life. It is a single cell that can give rise to progeny that differentiate into any of the specialized cells of embryonic or adult tissues.

~ Stewart Sell

The first successful regenerative medicine therapy occurred in 1956 when stem cells from the bone marrow of an identical twin were used to restore their sibling's bone marrow after they had undergone irradiation. The transplanted stem cells, capable of growing and differentiating into a number of various cell types, succeeded in achieving a complete remission of the sibling's leukemia by replenishing the cellular elements of their bloodstream.

At first stem cells were obtained from the bone marrow of normal donors, later they were obtained from stem cells mobilized into the peripheral bloodstream of a donor. And, around 1990, a third source of stem cells from umbilical cord blood was reported that facilitated the restoration of hematopoiesis. All of these stem cell sources are typically used to restore blood-forming cells but have also been used for non-hematopoietic disorders.

More recently, other sources of stem cells with the capability of restoring non-blood forming cells have been identified. These stem cell sources include embryonic stem cells, induced pluripotent stem cells (iPS) and pluripotent mesenchymal stromal cells (MSCs). The potential of these stem cells as treatment modalities to repair and replace defective cells in a variety of disease states are currently under study. In particular, there are numerous clinical trials exploring the potential of the MSC to treat disease states that involve inflammatory bowel disease, musculoskeletal injuries, liver damage, burns and skin injuries, and spinal cord injury.

Picture this; a world where medicine is designed not to heal, but to regenerate. Regenerative medicine is best described as new translational research competing to reach commercialization. It is fast becoming a part of our reality too, which is why it is attracting so much attention from the healthcare industry. It is also encouraging a new wave of multidisciplinary approaches to a variety of clinical applications. However, it still faces a plethora of challenges ahead before it reaches surgeries.

Stem cells possess enormous regenerative potential.
The potential applications are virtually limitless.

~ Kristin Comella

CHAPTER 2

THE BIGGEST BARRIER TO YOUR STEM CELL PRACTICE – THE X FACTOR

What is the X-Factor and Why is It So Important to You as a Chiropractor?

Trust is a firm belief in the reliability, truth, ability, or strength of someone. The definition seems very clear and straightforward, however for some putting trust into action is the equivalent of climbing Mount Everest with no gear, no supplies, and only one arm. Trust is fundamental to life. If you cannot trust in anything, life becomes intolerable—a constant battle against paranoia and looming disaster. You can't have relationships without trust, let alone good ones. Intimacy depends on it.

No matter what aspect of your life you're thinking about, trust is always a major factor. That could be in the family unit; the neighborhood; on the sporting field or in the workplace and especially in healthcare. Trust is vitally important to us on a variety of levels, from the importance that you trust the people around you in your everyday life to be the best and healthiest person you can be. People also fail to realize just how important trust is in the bigger picture, but events such as revolutions show just how far a little distrust in authority can go.

If we can trust wholeheartedly that a someone is there to support us in the toughest of times, it makes us feel that we have someone in our corner in life. What seemed daunting is now something that is manageable. We can more effectively take on the challenges of the world and come out better for it.

"The best marketing doesn't feel like marketing."

~ Tom Fishburne

When we trust someone, we allow ourselves to be vulnerable, we open up and share the truth of what resides within us, both good and bad. We share our greatest fears, our deepest uncertainties, and our greatest dreams. But without this elusive thing called trust, walls, barriers, and roadblocks stand in the way of connecting and creating that powerful feeling called trust.

What Are The Two Key Factors That Create Trust?

Based on the work of Stephen M R Covey, the author of The Speed of Trust, the essential components to developing trust are character and Competency.

Our character is who we are; our competence is what we can do. If we're strong in one area and weak in the other, we won't sustain trust in the long run. I might trust an individual with high character but low competence if I went on vacation and needed someone to watch my home because they're honest. But I may not trust them on a key project if they don't have a track record of performing. The reverse is true as well. Someone could be high in competence but low in character. They might get things done, but in doing so, they might also violate the beliefs and values of the agency. That lack of character will undermine trust and credibility. There are four cores of credibility.

Bringing it home with Chiropractic.

We as Chiropractors have high levels of perceived character. Meaning our intent, agenda, and our overall motive for the most part is aligned with the greater good of the patient. They feel our sincerity. They observe how we listen to their 10 minute story about their cat named Ava. Yet even with this deep desire to connect and to create a great sense of caring for the patient, we can't crack the ten percent utilization in this country. Why? Because Character is not enough for us. We need more than this. After all we are doctors, and we must balance the trust equation with the other half which is the competency portion.

"You can't be everything to everyone but you can be something to someone."

~ Drew Davis, Brandscaping

Competency is observed and measured based on the perceived skill, ability and overall sense of intelligence that we possess. Here's our problem – embedded within the degree of the medical doctor is prestige, respect, admiration, and a perception of above average intelligence. Most people are intimidated by a doctors intelligence, that is why few question the recommendations of their doctor. Would you like to know what we get in our degree? Do we get respect? Admiration? Prestige? None of this. What we have within our degree, is the right to do what we do without going to jail. THAT IS IT.

- **Integrity.** Integrity means honesty and that there is a very little gap between what we say and what we do. I liken it to the roots of a tree.

- **Intent.** Intent refers to your motive or agenda. The agenda that best builds credibility and trust is one of mutual benefit, where I want your win as much as I want my own. The intent is the trunk of the tree.

- **Capabilities.** Your capabilities is like the branches of the tree. By capabilities, I mean learning, growing, improving and staying relevant.

- **Credibility.** Credibility is the fruits of the tree, it is the results or your performance.

What Are The Components Of Character?

Trust is built over time as you follow through with the promises you make. Your credibility — the □uality or power of inspiring belief — grows in much the same way. The principles of trust and credibility are tightly linked and build on each other. In his book The Speed of Trust, Stephen M.R. Covey defines the "4 Cores of Credibility" as foundational elements that make you believable, both to yourself and to others. The first two cores deal with character, the second two with competence:

Integrity: Many e□uate integrity with honesty. While honesty is a key element, integrity is much more. It's integratedness, walking your talk and

"The cost of being wrong is less than the cost of doing nothing."

~ Seth Godin

being congruent, inside and out. It is having the courage to act in accordance with your values and beliefs. Most violations of trust are violations of integrity.

Intent: At the core of intent are motives, agendas and the resulting behavior. Trust grows when your motives are straightforward and based on mutual benefit — when you genuinely care not only for yourself but also for the people you interact with, lead or serve.

Capabilities: Your capabilities are the abilities you have that inspire confidence — your talents, attitude, skills, knowledge, and style. They are the means you use to produce results.

Results: Your results comprise your track record, your performance and getting the right things done. If you don't accomplish what you are expected to do it diminishes your credibility. On the other hand, when you achieve the results you promised, you establish a positive reputation of performing, of being a producer.

Each of these cores is vital to credibility. They work together to build trust. The strength of your character and competence e□uate to the strength of your leadership.

Why Are These Components So Important?

The character of a person refers to their morals, values, and qualities as a human being. It has nothing to do with physical traits or your upbringing. It is more closely tied to your personality. Your character defines who you are as a person and what you believe in. If you're a good person who has solid morals and values, you'll have a good character. If you're someone who has questionable morals, you may have a □uestionable character. It's that simple. Operating a Chiropractic office ethically, with integrity and honesty, represents a key component in attracting new patients.

"Marketing is really just about sharing your passion."

~ Michael Hyatt

Competency, Why Is This So Important?

Competency means that you can do something well. You are capable of performing a task or job effectively. Competency can include the knowledge and skills needed to solve a quadratic equation. Or, it can comprise the much larger and more diverse skill required to be a Chiropractor.

The reason writing a book on stem cell therapy is so damn important for us as chiropractors is because we bottom line have low status in healthcare. People are highly suspect of us, and skeptical of us as healthcare providers. Most patients don't even see us as doctors, they see us as quasi massage therapists/physical therapists. So when we are offering such highly specialized therapy such as Stem Cell Therapy, we must align ourselves with the authority and create a powerful identity as a trusted health care advisor.

When you write a book on Stem Cell Therapy, something changes, they no longer question your skills, or abilities, your legitimicay is not an issue anymore. You are seen as an authority, an expert, someone with above average intelligence, and in their mind they believe that they have found someone that can help them solve their problems. You need to remember that people are silently begging to be led to the promise land of a pain free life. They want to see you as their Moses so to speak, but there are too many charlatans out there that lean to much on Charisma, and not enough on competency. Remember, patients are silently begging to be led, but they need you to have Authority, not just Charisma.

"Make the prospect a more informed buyer with content."

~ Robert Simon

CHAPTER 3

THE REAL PROBLEM THAT CHIROPRACTORS HAVE

We as Chiropractors Don't Have a Problem with Educating Our Patients. We Have a Problem with Positioning

John is a chiropractor. Licensed. Down to earth. Knows the Nervous System, and the Spine like the back of his hands. He loves his patients so much so that he often goes out on a limb to please them. In essence, John is the best there is and his patients love him for this. The way he magically adjusts their spines is divine!

Yet, John sits daily by the window in his office, his gaze far off into the distance. His thoughts roam wildly as he struggles to grasp bits and pieces of what is clawing at his sanity. You see, John still lives below par. He still struggles to send his girls their monthly allowances on time. He is behind on some payments and in no time, the inevitable will come calling – irrelevance. Over the years, he had been given advice by friends and folks about how to matter in the chiropractic profession. He had attended seminars and conferences. He had honoured little events with his presence yet several years down the line, he still hadn't found that 'click' that said all would be well.

This is the dilemma that most chiropractors find themselves. They have done all possible to make sure that they mattered yet still, what they seek eludes them. They don't still get the recognitions and the speaking engagements, nor invites for reviews. This is the sad but true example of a typical   chiropractor.

"The importance of gratitude is never forgotten."

~ Deborah Lee

Communication is no problem. You as a chiropractor have no issues with communicating the right information to your patients. You always know what to tell them. After all, your time in school was no joke. In fact, you communicate and educate them so well that there is marked improvement in their individual lives as well as the care system. But why doesn't the present state of things get you the desired exposure you crave? It is simply because you have not mastered the art of positioning; of being in the best of positions at the right time.

Positioning defines where you and /or your product (item or service) stands in relation to others offering similar products and services in the marketplace as well as the mind of the consumer. This is saying that positioning defines where you as a chiropractor, offering chiropractic service(s) stands in relation to your fellow chiropractors in the chiropractic marketplace as well as the minds of your consumers (patients and others alike).

A good positioning makes your chiropractic treatments unique and makes your 'clients' consider using it as a thing of immense benefit to them what with a marketplace that is swarming with similar offerings.

A good positioning makes you stand out from the rest of the chiropractors. By so doing, it confers on you the ability to charge a higher price on your service and starve off competition from your peers. A good position in the market also allows you and affords you the opportunity to weather storms more easily.

Newspapers, magazines, newsletters and other forms of communication will help in getting you in position at all times but nothing compares to putting information in a book. A book though traditional has proven over time to be the best source of positioning power. Yes, those 400- or something pages of expert information is a sure bet to getting the kind of exposure you seek as a chiropractor. It's not all about the long hours you spend by patients' bedsides nor the amount of time you spend massaging a

"This is a learning process and sometimes you have to fall in order to learn things."

~ Christine Korda

crooked spine. It's in the amount of time you have spent in pouring value into a book; something people can read and relate to.

The advanced age has not in any way reduced the demand for expert knowledge. Humans by nature are always searching for ways to make sure that they never lack information. Little wonder everywhere is agog with 'do you know...' tags.

A book is an instant credibility booster for you. It is positioning and authority combo. They hardly get thrown away like business cards. With books, you can demonstrate your chiropractic genius and dexterity and show examples of your knowledge and experience. You are treated as a celebrity chiropractor.

Books never lie! They speak the minds of whoever has written them and this is the height of communication – when you can peruse through lines of text and your mind is able to feed fat on the nuggets of knowledge that pour endlessly.

Let us now dwell more on the author in you, who has been able to translate further, his expertise into producing a book on stem cell therapy. You have succeeded in putting all your knowledge within the confines of a book. How does this book help you gain good positioning in the marketplace that probably has hundreds of your colleagues and peers, with or without a publication?

Factually, writing books is an inefficient and ineffective way of making income. Your book on say, "Chiropractic of the 21st Century", falls under the non-fiction genre and as such, may not be the one to earn you a fat income. To profit from such a book, you have to let your book be a marketing tool for other services that is offered by you! We're talking about speeches, seminars, webinars and the whole nine yards. This is good positioning!

"Find your spirit, and no challenge will keep you from achieving your goals."

~ Christopher Penn

Any author, you, who succeeds at this has carefully positioned the book – that is, has *identified its target readers and their needs* – before putting down the words. In other words, this market position is very much a twin to the position that you as an author wish to hold in your chiropractic field.

Now, there abound in the marketplace, many physician-authors albeit 'chiropractor-authors' who write simply because there's something they are aching to say. They write the first book and go hunting for publishers and booksellers to figure out how to sell the thing. What they forget is that publishers are people who never make an offer on a book unless there is a confidence that they can reach intended audiences. It is up to you as the author to define these audiences.

It pays to position your book. Why? Because to write a book (like our fictitious one in the earlier paragraph) is to enter into a relationship with your readers, who will only like the book when they feel this relationship.

So, positioning is simply how you bring your readers into the larger picture and identify what they want you to give. So you see that the problem of we chiropractors is not educating our patients, it is in actually connecting with them on a level that transcends the simple healthcare personnel-patient dialogue.

How then do you go about positioning?

Positioning begins with your book title and a subtitle. There is nothing that grabs a reader's attention more than a catchy title. The title of your book must be short, pithy, easy-to-remember, and focuses on the unique selling point of what makes the book unique.

How do you explain why you are the best choice for their Stem Cell Therapy Needs? Your book does or better still, the contents of your book. Framing highlights in your illustrious career as a chiropractor will go a long way in fattening and cementing the way people perceive you.

Personally, I am very fond of strawberries and cream, but I have found that for some strange reason, fish prefer worms.

~ Dale Carnegie

Moreover, demonstrate your book's concrete benefits. Getting to educate is not a big deal, but what are the problems that your expert book addresses? How does your book help solve these problems? Specificity wins in such scenarios. Therefore, you must show how your book will appeal and endear readers albeit the media. A vital point is *don't try to position and make yourself or your book appeal to everyone! It weakens the message you preach!*

Go social! The social media offers immense benefits to getting the word out about you and your chiropractic enterprise. Even better is the fact that you have a book. Register your presence on various platforms, leveraging on the unique capabilities that they have to offer. In the long run, the market naturally opens up and readers gravitate towards the messages they have had you preach. You get more patients. You get more readers. You get a loyal fan base. You get huge publicity. You get referrals. All of these translating into building an authority which is your priority. Your bookless peers and competitors would cower in respect.

When the issues of positioning is solved, every other thing falls into place. Top of that list is the authority you now command as both a chiropractor and as an expert author. This new found authority means that you have literally become the best voice concerning matters that have to do with chiropractic. You speak and everybody listens for your words now carry a message that resonates loudly with the minds of your audiences, and that I'll say is the best form of influence you could ever get in a world that is always gravitating towards wells of knowledge. You get to quench the thirsts of many a people.

Summarily, every component of your positioning master plan should and must push out the same message in a myriad of ways, each one strengthening and deepening your message to the market. Getting online will help you be seen as an expert chiropractor. It's easier than you might think.

Marketing is no longer about the stuff that you make, but about the stories you tell.

~ Seth Godin

CHAPTER 4

WHY A BOOK IS BETTER THAN ANY OTHER MARKETING TOOL

Years back, a college degree was what you needed to be certified as strong professional in any field or profession. All you needed was to get into a college and come out well equipped with good grades and great understanding of your profession but the times have changed and a college degree doesn't suffice anymore. With the technological advanced world we are where anyone can get a degree anywhere in the world , it became necessary for something else to separate the men from the boys, there was a need for people to set themselves apart from the millions of professionals in each field. There are a lot of ways people go about it these days but one very effective one his by individuals writing a book. A book is a sign of credibility and authority; it is quite rare and reliable, especially amidst chiropractors. Here is what I tell people, to be a thought leader, write a book.

I know you are not convinced enough yet on why you should start hitting on your computer keyboard in the name of writing a book, how does it really affect your income? How does it help my patients? How does it make me different from every other person out there in this line of work? These thoughts are legitimate and serve as the basis of this book, why you need to be an authority in the profession.

Have you noticed the caliber of people media outlets call whenever they want a comment on an issue? An expert in that field right? And what metrics do they use to determine if someone is an expert? Many times because they wrote a book. Writing is a sure-fire point of authority and credibility. You would usually hear something like "On the show today is

Success is not final; failure is not fatal: It is the courage to continue that counts.

~Winston S. Churchill

Jim, Jim is the author of so & so book and he will be discussing the causes of so & so with us" Sounds familiar? They didn't just pick Jim because he is a chiropractor, they picked him to discuss with because they see him as an expert in the field, as a credible point of the profession. Many times, we have a lot of better chiropractors than Jim but because they do not put their knowledge out, they are never going to be called.

If you want visibility as a chiropractor or any professional at that, if you yearn for that media coverage, then you should write a book that puts you out as an expert in the field, doing this makes media coverage a little more easier to get. The media do not want to talk to random people in professions, they want to talk to industry experts, and how best do they judge expertise? By the books they have written on the subject.

I have a mutual friend who made millions off her book even though she sold fewer than 1,000 copies. How's that? She wrote on a hot topic at that time which was pop-up retail and after that a lot of media outlet that were focused on retail wanted to have a session with her. She was now an expert in the vey much sought after field.

My friend didn't necessarily have to write a book for a large audience, she wrote the book for a selected target audience. Even as you read this , you do not know a lot of people that want to open up a pop-up retail outlet but because she had a carved out target market for herself which was new then by the way, there was rarely any established opinion maker yet, her name pops up first whenever anyone needed anything in that expertise. She had the knowledge, she put herself out and she became better for it.

Using the example of my friend above as an inter-industry example is only to prove that this model works around all industries and fields of life. Writing a book gives your personal brand a boost, it gives your person the "Trust Factor" and in marketing, once you are trusted, you have won the very first battle with your audience. So how does a book make people trust you? Why is Facebook not a better marketing tool than a book? Why don't I just create a Vlog or a blog to talk professionally?

Make it simple, but significant.

~ Don Draper

Interestingly, Amazon is the number three most popular search engine in the world just after Google and YouTube, and to even make it more interesting, it is the number one search engine for professionals; yes it does rank higher than LinkedIn. When experts or people with a voice in a field are being searched for, just like the media, they almost always usually want the person who "wrote a book" on the particular topic. Having a very good book like as been stated earlier allows people to know exactly who you are, how you can be of help to them, and your book even brings them closer to you. Writing a book is the best marketing tool you could ever use to build and grow your brand and gain patients trust.

I once read of the experience of an entrepreneur who started Book In A Box, he said he realized he was erecting a massive building without a proper blueprint, he and his team knew they needed to learn how to scale a company successfully. He said he went on Amazon to read books on the said topic. He read one written by Cameron Herold titled Double Double which helped him understand his subject matter. He got in contact with Cameron, and he became not only his coach but also a business partner.

Out there, there are a whole lot of people that could take two to three hours of their time to teach him how to scale his business, they might even call it a master class, but when his session with them is done, he will most likely need to fall back to a book to guide him as he practiced. He read Cameron's book and not only did he enjoy it and understood what he was looking for, he reached out to him and they became business partners and that will be because he trusted his judgment.

There is rarely a better tool for marketing than word of mouth. When people you trust normally tell you to subscribe to something, you are going to most likely to listen. Any method or means that gets other people to talk about you and your business is the best marketing tool possible for you. For chiropractors, a book enables word of mouth better than almost anything else.

The aim of marketing is to know and understand the customer so well the product or service fits him and sells itself.

~ Peter F. Drucker

Unlike video and audio adverts where people see or hear things or people that inform them of the creator or the brand, a book allows for readers to create you. They form their opinion totally from the words they read and if your book is half good, they make you into a half god, you have shaped their perception of yourself and your profession. They trust you, be it a patient or a fellow professional.

A book allows you to put your story into people's minds and then in their mouths, so when they go all out to talk about you, they are saying what you want them to say out there about your book, ideologies and your person. If you end up publishing a very good book, people will speak of your terms, phrases, and ideologies to other people, they speak your language in their own words.

This is the idea which authors should have in mind when they are writing and positioning the framework of their books. Authors or potential authors should imagine someone at a dinner or cocktail party who had read their book, and they start a conversation with someone who happens to be in their potential audience. What would you want them telling people about you? your ideologies? Your knowledge and impact? Imagine what you want them to say to the other person, you should write that and people will help you market it just like this.

If you can understand the scenario narrated above that it could naturally happen between two people, you can almost get to construct how your book should go from these conversations. If you write a book that is of immense value to a certain group of people, there is a high probability they will want to talk about your book to someone else who is in their purview, this is because they get to be an authority, they get to be a voice on the matter you have iterated in your book. This is exactly how word of mouth works and once someone has heard about you, it is easy for them to pick up your book, research on you, and interact with your work. Books bring to you clients, it is called content marketing on steroids.

You can't sell anything if you can't tell anything.

~ Beth Comstock

I have found myself read some books and go ahead to tell people in my circle to go get it, I even end up buying as gift for some of them, as much as technology is fast changing our lives, some of the underlining elements of technology will only be built on and not destroyed, books are part of them. For professionals who do not want to become stagnant in their fields, books are very important. For chiropractors, it is even more important to keep on reading at each point of their lives. Technology is breaking grounds in medicine and surgery daily, new ways to approach treating patients are being unearthed daily. It is expedient to stay in touch with the learning process and even more interesting to be the teacher of the new school chiropractors.

The key is, no matter what story you tell, make your buyer the hero.

~ Chris Brogan

CHAPTER 5

THE MILGRAM EXPERIMENT AND THE POWER OF AUTHORITY

One of the most important and popular studies carried out on human obedience in psychology was done by Stanley Milgram, a renowned psychologist at Yale University. He conducted this experiment while focusing on the conflict between obedience to authority and humans personal conscience.

The Milgram experiment was used to explain some of the horrors that happened at the concentration camps during World War 2, where the Jews, homosexuals, gypsies, slavs and other enemies of the movement were slaughtered by the Nazis. Many of the war-criminals that were interrogated after the World War 2 claimed they were just pawns following orders and as so could not be held responsible for their actions. Was it that the Germans were pure evil and cold-hearted, or was it just a group following orders of their master which could happen to any of us if we were in the same condition?

In 1961, Stanley Milgram put out an advertisement in the New Haven Register saying *"We will pay you $4 for one hour of your time,"* the copy went on to read *"500 New Haven men to help us complete a scientific study of memory and learning."*

Over the next two years, people came into his laboratory in their hundreds for the learning and memory study that was advertised, it is good to note that it turned into something different very fast. While the person performing the experiment watches, the volunteer who was called "the teacher" would recite a number of words to their partner, "the learner,"

Marketing used to be about making a myth and telling it. Now it's about telling a truth and sharing it.

~ Marc Mathieu

who was tightened up to an electric-shock machine in another room. Every time the learner made a mistake in reciting the words from the teacher, a shock of increasing intensity was delivered on the learner, which started from like 15 volts and was labelled "slight shock" on the equipment it was disseminated from) increasing all the way up to about 450 volts which read "severe shock". Even though some teachers were horrified at what was being requested of them to do, they stopped the experiment quite early, ignoring the experiment supervisor's request for them to go on; while some others continued the task and used up to 450 volts, ignoring the learner's loud plea for mercy and his yelling and warning about his terrible heart condition, the learner then falls alarmingly silent. In the widely accepted part of this experiment, 65 percent of the people went all the way with the punishments unleashed on the learner.

The teachers and learners didn't know that the shocks unleashed were not real till they came out of the laboratory, they did not know that the cries of pain from the other room were pre-recorded, and that the learner who was the voice of the whole experiment was a railroad auditor whose name was Jim McDonough, he was very well alive and unharmed in a separate room. All the participants were equally naïve that they were being used to prove the claim from Milgram that would soon make him very famous: His claim was that "ordinary people, under the direction of an authority, would obey any order that they were given, even to the extent of torture"

Milgram's experiment proved that ordinary people are very likely to follow orders if they are meted out by people in authority, It further proved that people can go as far as of killing innocent people to satisfy authority. In all humans, obedience to authority is embedded in all of us from cradle, we have been taught to be submissive. Even the strongest rebels become submissive to at least one figure in authority.

People are more inclined to obey orders from other individuals if they see their authority as morally correct or if there is a legal backing. The response to authority is learned in different kinds of situations, for example in the

Good marketers see consumers as complete human beings with all the dimensions real people have.

~ Jonah Sachs

family, school, and workplace. Both the legal and philosophical aspects of obedience to authority are of enormous importance, but they give very little details about how most people behave in real life situations.

In other words, the power of authority can be seen in the average number of followers to your cause, the average number of readers who have no choice than to 'follow your orders'. Why? Because you have given them no other choice.

By reason of the fact that you have poured your expert chiropractic self into your book(s), what people now see is you, manifested through such manuscript. Yes! That is authority! Authority begets compliance – compliance to rules and dictates, compliance to laws and statutes. There is no better way to assert authority than by making your audience believe that the contents you carry and have been able to document (in book form that is) are worth every ounce of respect and eventual deference they are willing to surrender, because in all, Milgram's experiment brings to the fore the unbelievable fact that *"the physical presence of an authority figure dramatically increases compliance"*.

Another inference to be drawn from the results of Milgram's experiments is the fact that all participants assumed that the experimenter was a competent expert. Riding on the backs of the events that transpired in the other room, it was very easy for the participants to think so. You see, momentary situational pressures can exert a significant level of influence on people's behaviour as Milgram had pointed out. The ability for your audience to see you as a competent chiropractor is borne not out of the fact that they are being coerced into thinking so, it is the simple fact that they know so! Every word in your book should carry a weight that resonates with a particular set of people on different scales and in differing degrees.

Your work as a chiropractor writing albeit your work as an author places the power of creation at your fingertips. You sculpt words in such a way that your audience practically feel that it is absolutely essential for them to

If you have more money than brains, you should focus on outbound marketing. If you have more brains than money, you should focus on inbound marketing.

~ Guy Kawasaki

resonate with every swing of a pendulum that you have thus set in motion. The plain truth is that most often, the audience have no way of really authenticating whether or not all is perfect, they just "assume" it is! These assumptions are not at all bad. In fact, it is based on these same assumptions that the audience starts embarking on the eventual journey on roads to belief and trust. Yes, books can give that kind of power!

The lack of information which has now become a major tear in the world fabric is another reason to leverage on asserting the authority you have as an expert chiropractor. There are two sides to this huge coin. Everywhere people turn to, they reek of ignorance. The fact that they don't know doesn't seem to bother them and they trudge on in their obvious folly, being bent to the wiles of that which they are ignorant of. On the other divide are the hungry audience who always want a piece of every new cake. They seek knowledge and would do anything to get it – anything!

Milgram's experiment involved 'shock administration' between a 'teacher' and 'student'. Students getting shocked was as a result of information being fed to the teacher, who then translated it the best way he could and the result was a student getting shocked or not.

When you step in as an author to fill the gaps caused by a lack of necessary information, you wield the power to twist and turn the hearts of people. You put yourself in a position where these people – your audience – rely solely on you to make their mind decisions. That power is raw! It is the power of authority, only wielded by those who have what it takes to fill the voids of a lack of information.

So, being an author is the shortest route to being a symbol of authority. People simply assume you have a lot to offer and would not mind going the extra mile to make sure they are first partakers of the fruits your tree is bearing.

Economics also teaches of demand and supply as the ultimate exchange. Demand begets supply and vice versa. It is the same way it is with the

Martin Luther King did not say 'I have a mission statement'.

~ Simon Sinek

creation of worthy content. As a chiropractor who has worn the new shoes of an author, the eventual authority that your book exudes largely will depend on the demands for it. Such demands only come when it is obvious that every chiropractic knowledge and information you have poured out into it is worth it. We have earlier asserted that compliance is an inherent trait in humans. How strong this trait is, is a function of how much demands the audience have placed.

Your book must be compelling. So much so its contents engaging that the demand for the information therein increases. When demand increases, the people's response (supply) also increases. All these are a result of the authority that your book has been able to exert. Nobody bows to what does not tower over it! Your compelling content gives you as a chiropractor the power to tower above those with a hunger for the information you possess as well as your bookless counterparts – peers or competition. This is influence! This is power! This is authority! And none other than books wield this kind of power.

What helps people, helps business.

~ Leo Burnett

CHAPTER 6

A STEM CELL THERAPY BOOK AS THE ULTIMATE LEAD GENERATION TOOL

We are all familiar with the conventional business card. That 3 by 2 inch glossy card that carries all the details of what you do as a chiropractor and the other services (related or not) it offers, as well as contact information. It is often said that a book is the new business card. But before we delve right into the chapter, we have to define the obvious terms.

Let's stroll through the obvious questions. What are leads? What is lead generation? How does a book help you generate leads?

A lead is a person who has expressed interest in your service. He is a qualified potential 'buyer' who has an intention to have a taste of your service and has reached out in communication to do so. In other words, a random call, text or correspondence from someone who has had access to your contact information, doesn't count as a lead.

Lead generation is simply a marketing method that involves the capturing, stimulation and subsequent nurturing of the interest of strangers in the services that you offer. It is a process that helps you cement the right relationships with leads that your services have helped you gather. It is the method of getting inquiries from potential customers.

Lead generation could be achieved in various forms. Your book is one of them. Other types of lead generation content include but are not limited to courses, trials, demos, contests, checklists, podcasts, slideshare presentations, templates and webinars.

The best marketing doesn't feel like marketing.

~ Tom Fishburne

You wonder how a book – your book on the principles and practice of chiropractic will help you get business authority? Read on.

The earlier chapters have buttressed the fact that as an author, whatever content you choose to put in your book should be compelling enough to warrant a heavy demand from your audiences. More so, people should be able to create and define you by mere taking a look at the contents of your book.

When writing a book, you have the opportunity to turn it into the best tool for maximal lead generation by incorporating and embedding several endearing elements of the chiropractic practice all of which make for a wider reading and a subsequent appreciation for the knowledge you have been able to pour out and pass across.

When your readers connect with you and are able to feed off the passion you've been able to put in, it is only natural that they want more of it – more of you. It gets to a point that they would graduate into connecting with you on a personal note – outside of the book(s). These readers, who have become highly motivated individuals by reason of your content, will go to many lengths to seek you out all in a bid to follow you, hire you, be mentored by you or even be partnered with.

Lead generation as asserted is a core marketing process. It deals with how to market the information you have packaged into your book. Information on how chiropractic employs a variety of non-surgical treatments and how the spine and nerves are at the centre of healing. How to drive readership and sales. There are strategies that must be put in place if your book is going to get you the leads you seek. These strategies must be in line with the latest trends in the market. It is of no use trying to employ outdated tactics in dealing with an evolved civilization.

One sure way your book can help generate leads is by encouraging your readers to engage and go deeper with you. How?

Good marketing makes the company look smart. Great marketing makes the customer feel smart.

~ Joe Chernov

Invite them to join your email list.

Your email list is a simple and natural way of bringing your readers closer into your network. By so doing, you give them the privilege to continue engaging with you on a more personal level. By inviting them to sign up for your email list right within the book, you are invariably telling them that you have seen the love they have for you and are willing to give yourself for free. With this list, you give them the opening to keep up with updates, news, content, events and new books that may interest them.

More so, people naturally respond to invitations and calls to action. A reach out to them by email lists shows that you not only are concerned with driving your sales or promoting your brand but are also interested in their success. This deepens their connection with you and in no time, your leads base increases.

Another sure way of using your book to generate leads is sending out invitations for an online class or webinar. Webinars are the internet equivalent of live seminars. Yes, your audience are loving you via your book. You can take it up a notch further by inviting them to an online class or webinar where you give them the opportunity to witness you live. They get to connect on a more personal level, asking questions and getting answers. No reader who has been 'hooked' on your print copy will pass on this opportunity.

One of the most direct and result-yielding of the lead generating methods is an invitation to a strategy session. This has proven over time to be the best method of converting your readership into clientele. What are strategy sessions? They are sessions that provide insight and discovery. People get to know you better. A well thought out and executed strategy session can eventually lead to offers.

In the same vein, you could as an author organize live events in frequencies that appeal to you. Inviting your readers to such events will guarantee that

Even when you are marketing to your entire audience or customer base, you are still simply speaking to a single human at any given time.

~ Ann Handley

they get an opportunity to meet you in person as the author and expert they look up to.

Summarily, underlying all these strategies is the assumption that your book and the information contained therein is enough to convince people to buy from you. Writing a book isn't enough for any of these strategies to be effective. In all, what will guarantee the efficacy of these strategies is the fact that they create connections with the readers of your book if and only if the ideas have got them engaged.

If your ship doesn't come in, swim out to meet it!

~ Jonathon Winters

CHAPTER 7

HOW YOUR STEM CELL THERAPY BOOK WILL GET YOU SPEAKING ENGAGEMENTS

Having a book is one of the best ways to land a speaking engagement. Event organizers often times gravitate towards resource persons who have had a book published. Not only that, there are very high probabilities that they get to pay more.

Better yet, being the author of a book will get you invited to speak to bodies that are not too 'welcoming' for example professional associations, conferences, and so on. Organisers of these kinds of events (who also have their audiences) are wary of just anybody coming to grace their podiums.

As an author, you might have probably been schooled in the notion that public speaking isn't your forte – after all, you are a writer, not a speaker...right? This is not entirely true. Once you put a book out there – a book that matters that is – you have the best chance of standing out from the humongous crowd, eventually grabbing the attention of planners who require speaking services.

There are myths that circulate about why writing a book cannot earn you speaking engagements albeit riding on the back of chiropractic. The truth remains that everyone has that inherent trait to seek after the best stuff, especially as it relates to information and as it relates to them and their preferences. Information is power and people would do anything to wield such power. There has been no other way to explore sources of this power than experts and gurus (like you) who have a store of information – books, which they have made available.

Your time is limited, so don't waste it living someone else's life.

~ Steve Jobs

Public speaking is an incredibly fascinating endeavour. There is nothing quite like it. That feeling you get as you stand in the middle of an amphitheatre, a camera trained on you, blurting out words, phrases and sentences with the dexterity of a wordsmith, all in an attempt to convey certain rehearsed information.

Your qualification to speak in gatherings of chiropractors (or otherwise) ultimately depends on several factors, chief of which is EXPERT KNOWLEDGE in that field of chiropractic. Come to think of it; of all the other available speakers who are obviously better and could dexterously present such topic, why you? Perhaps you've earned a degree (or two) on the subject. Maybe you have rubbed shoulders with the host and lobbied for the slot.

I have come to find out that the best qualifications comes from the fact that YOU HAVE A MATERIAL OUT THERE – A BOOK, which contains a truckload of relevant information that people are aching to hear. Information that lays bare the skeleton of chiropractic as a discipline. We have discussed the fact that the lack of information coupled with a people's growing thirst for such 'elusive' information would make them do anything to fill that void. The expert knowledge you have gathered over the years as a chiropractor, poured into a manuscript and consequently a book - your book, have put you on a pedestal few steps higher than your bookless peers who still revel in the fatness of their mental archives.

Speaking engagements help you as an author, build an enviable and loyal fan base. A network of loyalists and believers. And believe it when I tell you that with such loyalty, you could get the whole world on a platter of gold.

What are we talking about? Your books will only get you speaking engagements if and only if readers can feel the passion you have poured into the creation of such content. This same passion that has made you succeed as the go-to chiropractor. When audiences feel your deep and unwavering connection to the topic(s) you preach, it stirs up in them a

Business has only two functions – marketing and innovation.

~ Peter Drucker

desire for motivation. Positive testimonials from one or two audiences floats around and like wildfire, spreads in the form of referrals which will ultimately land you several high-profile speaking engagements. That's the power of testimonials!

Your books boost your reputation as a chiropractor, especially with the media. You can become the person that the media calls for expert opinion on chiropractic and you can leverage this reputation into regular appearances.

Your book will also get you speaking engagements when it is created to impress. As an author, writing a book about the practices of chiropractic is not the ultimate height of it. Whatever you have decided to write must be transformational, giving people the kind of answers they seek. No good comes from writing a book which hoards information. Yes, there are authors who are scared of giving away 'all their secrets'. By so doing, they drive away the same people who would eventually be their tickets to limelight. Some people are such that simply reading is just all for them. It isn't the same as listening and experiencing you in person.

Another variation of testimonials exists. This is endorsements. These are forms of advertising, often written or spoken statements that use famous personalities to drive awareness of your service. Endorsements simply show that whatever service you are rendering, in this case, your book, is supported and approved. A clutch of endorsements on your book cover can also be a huge help. They position you as a respected expert, and that can only help you gain the speaking opportunities that you desire. Look to high profile clients who have been guests on your massage tables and chairs. Let them endorse you through your book.

Promoting yourself as a speaker comes with a clause also – that you sell your speaking within your book. Sound familiar? The sure way to lose credibility as a trusted expert is to give people the impression that you cannot speak. Once they form this impression, it becomes hard for them to actually recognize your worth as a trusted authority on chiropractic. In

Have the end in mind and every day make sure your working towards it.

~ Ryan Allis

essence, your book will get you speaking engagements when your readers can see and sift out the speaker in you. By leveraging on this quality you have so expertly introduced, the probabilities of gracing speaking platforms increases.

In addition, getting lucrative and appealing speaking engagements as an authored chiropractor is largely about how well written your eventual book is and what you do once that book is written. With the right strategies in place, speaking engagements will roll in one after the other. Let your book(s) build excitement in your readers. That's the ultimate goal of any and every author. By getting to the point of having a publishable/published material, you have already mastered the arts of writing, editing as well as market research. These skills are what event planners seek when scouring for speakers for their various engagements.

Audio is fast gaining popularity with the increase in advancing technology. Many folk out there don't want to seem too 'traditional' by carrying hardcover books in their laps. Leverage on your identity as a chiropractor to invest value in your book. Use necessary equipment to make an audio recording of your book.

So, your status as an author chiropractor will get you speaking engagements, then your book acts as the best 'trap' to get people onto your list of leads, which when worked on will open you to the many outlets that flows with authority.

The function of leadership is to produce more leaders, not more followers.

~ Ralph Nader

CHAPTER 8

HOW TO USE YOUR STEM CELL THERAPY BOOK TO GET FREE PUBLICITY

Readers are like hungry journalists, looking for that perfect story that will land them a Pulitzer. As a book author, this simply means that you are in the best position to create content that people are actually hungry for. As an author, you matter! You are always in the best position to give people what they want, what they crave, their addiction. Exposure is key to book sales and consequently authority mining.

Note this important notion about free publicity. Book promotion or publicity is designed to get people to find your book, and not, to find people to get your book. This is very true as your grasp of this statement will go a long way in determining how well you play your game of getting or securing reasonable promotions for your book.

There is always a publicity angle to every endeavour. You have to give to get. Your writing of content about chiropractic is the give part. Publicity caters for the get. Publicity is often overlooked as a primary marketing tool to gain the much needed attention and interest in your chiropractic service. The best move you can make as chiropractor-author is seeking to garner publicity using the same service (chiropractic) you have so lovingly and painstakingly put out there.

Getting free publicity means making sure that the information you have put into words gets the necessary and desired attention from people who resonate with every point you have made. If there is no publicity, obscurity is inevitable. What better way to get the word out there than by leveraging on various channels that aid exposure - a book, your book being one of

Paying attention to simple little things that most men neglect makes a few men rich.

~ Enry Ford

them. Getting into the media is very easy as an author than as any other individual.

Authority creation by being an author is dependent on whether or not that influence gets to the right circles. What is authority if its influence is not felt across divides? Know it that the society places a great value on authors more so, an author who is an accomplished chiropractor. It is no coincidence that the word "authority" starts with "author". This means that – *ceteris paribus* – your potential clients, your leads and customers are more likely to choose you because you are an author and a chiropractor all in one. That notwithstanding, if the word doesn't go out there that you are one, as earlier said, obscurity is the next rung on the ladder.

The power that lies within the covers of your book require the best forms of exposure. Your identity as a chiropractor will go a long way in giving a boost that will eventually grant you the well-deserved authority as an author.

Publicity takes various forms. It could be through the more ancient means or through the more conventional methods. Radios, TVs, newspapers and the whole nine yards. Whichever form of publicity is decided upon all boils down to the fact that content begets exposure. You wouldn't go about publicity if there has not been an actual demand for your content, would you?

How then do you use your book(s) to get free publicity?

One of the best and trusted ways of going about publicity is to engage the services of book review sites. These are sites that have made it their business to do a thorough rundown or critique of the contents of your book(s). They are the refining flames of whatever information you have put down in the pages of your book. Should your book pass this test, you are well on your way to amassing more readership. Your background as a chiropractor opens you more to certain technicalities about which you have

Formal education will make you a living; self-education will make you a fortune.

~ Jim Rohn

ample knowledge about. Once reviewers can pick and point to such, positive reviews are well on the way and guess what tags along – exposure.

For one, these review sites base their criticisms on personal taste. In such cases, it is very imperative that your reputation as a chiropractor matches whatever expectations they have in their minds. Anything short of impressive puts you at risk of a discredit and this in all ramifications is bad for building that power of authority. More so, you can ask readers for their reviews of your book and how much value(s) they got. These honest reviews go a long way in boosting your reputation as a chiropractor who is to be reckoned with.

Another way of generating free publicity is to search for bloggers in your select genre who perform and are accepting books for review. Bloggers are the next big thing when it comes to leveraging the internet as a tool for publicity. These individuals are bounty hunters of information. For a field as 'low laying' as chiropractic, they sure will be willing to get their hands on relevant information that will further drive traffic to the sites yet still at the same time, making sure the word gets out there about you and the values you are contributing. Build a relationship by engaging with them via various communication channels. By so doing, they will start paying the necessary attention to you. In the long run, this will pay off.

If you want to be more daring, you could also go the way of engaging bookstores and libraries, all in an effort to drive your reputation. The plan is to make sure that the availability of your content is a driving force to patronage. Going this route is a sure way of getting the kind of readership that could translate to the millions. Whether in hardcopy formats or not, resource materials on chiropractic are in demand. These bookstores and libraries make sure your book and its value is made available.

The best and sure-fire way to get publicity using your book is to treat the book like a business. It is obvious that no one would care about your book more than you do. In the same vein, no one is going to care for you more than you do. As chiropractors, there is always this notion from certain

Success is walking from failure to failure with no loss of enthusiasm.

~ Winston Churchill

quarters that the field is of little or no relevance. Going up against such notion means going the extra mile to make sure that threatening rumours don't spill over into soiling the reputation you have built in the hearts and minds of some loyal fans and clients.

You are first a chiropractor before your baptism into the writing world. Everything you do in the name of getting free publicity should reflect this idea. People should look at you and not see a hungry writer or author. They should see first the individual in you, the chiropractor who is a friend to his patients and clients, who is a lover of the care system, who above all is largely concerned with giving value. Only by doing this do you open the way to getting form such people – getting commendations, accolades, visits as well as partnerships.

You can gain free publicity using your books as leverage by going to conventions aimed at readers, *not authors*. By attending such gatherings, you get to speak on panels and meet people, making friends. This is promoting yourself to people who may not otherwise have heard about you – and who will now be interested in picking up your book, and possibly refer friends.

Remember that it is not really about the monetary returns. It is about the power of authority that you as an individual gets from your book. In other words, free publicity should be aimed at yourself first. Your book tows the line. Creating business cards is a handy hack to pushing yourself out there. It helps you, the chiropractor (and not the author) stay in touch. It is a cheap way of sharing contact information.

Sometimes, the best free publicity you can get as a chiropractor through your book comes from friends within the chiropractic circles. Yes, seeming competitor and enemies. This is a very thinly explored option by many chiropractor-authors. They hide behind the fact that nobody is to be trusted and so keep their books and values to a select few who may or may not help drive exposure and recognition. Getting publicity is a lot of work and the more hands you get, especially from those who have witnesses

Courage is being scared to death, but saddling up anyway.

~ John Wayne

first-hand your competencies, the better publicity you get, the more success achieved and the more influence exerted.

Advertising is only evil when it advertises evil things.

~ David Ogilvy

CHAPTER 9

HOW TO USE YOUR STEM CELL THERAPY BOOK AS YOUR ULTIMATE REFERRAL MARKETING TOOL

To avoid the "I have 2000 copies of my new book sitting in my garage, I just need to find people to buy them" conundrum, you should think about marketing even before you begin to write. Write a good book review for your book so you will have readers who will be willing to read it when it is eventually published.

However, the best type of marketing for chiropractic books is Referral marketing.

Referral marketing, or word of mouth, simply is people buying a product based on someone else's opinion, most times someone close to them. Referral marketing is an important part of any business, and knowing the basics of it will go a long way in mobilizing people to purchase your book as soon as it is published.

The best way to sell in any marketplace is through word of mouth. When you have faith in other people, and they tell you to purchase a product, you purchase because of the faith you have in them. Anything that lifts your status up in the marketplace is a tool for marketing. One of them is writing a book, and word of mouth is a perfect marketing tool.

According to a report by the Word of Mouth Marketing Association, more than 2 billion conversations about brands take place every day. This means that our society talks about a lot about the products they enjoy, and they also talk about the companies who offer these services too. Hence, if the

Referrals aren't given easily. If you don't take the time to establish credibility, you're not going to get the referral. People have to get to know you. They have to feel comfortable with who you are and what you do.

~ Ivan Misner

referral marketing route is to be used, you will know that your book, and you especially will be much talked about. 65% of all new opportunities come from referrals, according to a survey by the New York Times. That means of every three people, two have bought products because the products were recommended to them.

To bring it closer to home, a recent finding by Nielsen revealed that people are four times more likely to purchase a product if it was referred by a friend. These statistics prove that referral marketing can be an effective tool through which your book can be used to gain authority.

A book puts your ideas into people's mouths and minds, using your own words. As people talk about your book, and you, it will look like you are speaking to their minds through your book. What will define you as an author is when your book quotes and ideas are been repeated in chiropractic gatherings, and seminars and conferences. It shows that people are beginning to recognize you and see you as an expert in your field.

Often, this mindset is used to prime the minds of authors when they are writing. They are asked to imagine a random person in an organized setting, e.g. a dinner party who has read your book, having a conversation with another guest at the party about your book. The authors are then told to imagine what the people holding the conversations would talk about, or to put in context, what the writers want them to talk about.

What the above does is to help you create a narrative for how your book will be read by people, and how a typical referral marketing conversation should go. It should be imagined in a way that the other party that hadn't read your book will return home with so many questions in their minds, and they won't be satisfied until they've read your book, and indirectly until they find its writer.

If you write a book that changes the lives of people, they will inadvertently discuss your book with anybody who cares to listen, especially with people

People influence people. Nothing influences people more than a recommendation from a trusted friend. A trusted referral influences people more than the best broadcast message. A trusted referral is the Holy Grail of advertising.

~ Mark Zuckerberg

who need the same solutions as them. It makes them look good because they are speaking with much knowledge. It makes you look good because you are becoming popular.

As a chiropractor speaking with authority, your book should the readers what chiropractic means to you, the writer. You are hoping to sell yourself through your book; the best way to do that is to be unique. Being unique entails writing about your own experiences, about something that you do but others in your field don't do as good as you. For a chiropractor, it's choosing to focus on a particular aspect of chiropractic.

There are many self-help books out there that seem to draw knowledge from Chiropractic but are not. They don't even quote any chiropractic book; it's all jumbled together and pushed out. Google "alternative treatment to headaches" or "3 steps to perfect health without using drugs" and you get a lot of results from writers who don't know chiropractic in any way.

Everyone is looking for some expertise, for people who really know their thing, and that's why writing a book is the first step to selling your skills as a chiropractor. When you start the writing process, think about what you want to focus on in the book. You need to consider who will read your book, why they will read it, and what you will focus on.

You should also think about your patients. They are the best people to know how good your services are. And probably giving them your book for free will prove to them how highly you think of them. They are your first line of referral marketing. It will be better if your leverage on them.

Factors that affect referral marketing include the following:

1. Precision Targeting

If you have ever tried to advertise on Google or Facebook Ads, and have had the experience of losing money, then you will realize that many times,

Referrals are very powerful. When I refer you, I give a little bit of my reputation away. If you do a good job, my friend that hired you is pleased. But if you do a bad job, that reflects badly on me. People forget that.

~ Ivan Misner

there's a method to advertising. A good marketing process includes two important things; a good message and precision targeting. Fortunately for you, your book will have a good message, while Referral marketing will produce the precision targeting.

Word of mouth marketing is much more precise with its targeted marketing because people tend to give tips and advice to friends and members of their family. Referral marketing ensures that information about your book spreads faster than even other marketing styles.

2. Trust

Trust is important when you're trying to convince someone to buy a product. If we don't trust people, we would not listen to their advice.

The last time a salesman tried to sell a drug to you, you probably had doubts about his motivations. Is he selling the drug because he believes the drug works or his motivation is the commission he will receive from the sales? However, with your friends and family, you don't have such conundrum because you trust them. Trust also includes your favorite blog, or your favorite health website trying to sell a product to you on their platforms.

Over time, it has been shown that many trust their friends and family over believing in paid adverts and billboards, even the most beautiful adverts and billboards.

Here are other types of referral networks. The other party does not matter. The only thing that matters is that the person receiving the opinion trusts these networks.

i)   Friends/Family

ii) News Publications

Consumers are taking ownership of brands, and their referral power is priceless.

~ Erik Qualman

iii) Customer Reviews and Opinions Posted Online

iv) Influencer Opinions (Bloggers, Social Media Influencers)

v) Testimonials

3. Reach and Acceleration

Before, marketing reach was measured by the number of people you meet face to face to sell your products. However, with the advent of the internet, and blogging, reach is now measured by the number of people who visit a particular website at a particular time. If you decide to market your book on a blog, regular visitors on that blog will see the book every time they log into the website. The Internet gives speed to marketing reach.

70% of consumers give more credibility to consumer-created reviews and peer recommendations than professionally-written content.

~ Reevo

CHAPTER 10

HOW WRITING A STEM CELL THERAPY BOOK CREATES THE 'WOW' EFFECT WITH YOUR PATIENTS

As a chiropractor, your first responsibility is your vocation; the second are your patients. If you want to be an author, by writing a book on stem cell therapy, then you also have to factor in your patients. At the end of the day, you are writing the book for people who could be your patients. You know what to do; you have to 'wow' them.

As a Doctor, there's no greater referral than patients who are already in your care, and who have experienced some of the advice you are putting in your book. They know what it is about, and hence, their experiences should also be part of your story. However, moral ethics requires that you ask for their permission before you put their testimonials in your book.

Your patients, who are your 'Superfans' are already impressed. You, as a professional chiropractor, are taking their words as an evidence. It also shows that you are not bluffing. It helps to, in a way, manage expectations. Your new potential patients, after reading your book, know what to expect from you through the testimonials. Do not be different from who you say you are in your book; exceed that. Let the book be the least of what you can do. The whole purpose of writing a book is to advertise your knowledge and expertise and to make everyone know about you, thereby increasing patient enrollment. Don't defeat that purpose by performing less than you promised during consultations.

You also need to look at the demographic you want to 'wow'. For example, if through research, and Doctor-patient relations, you have found out that

Creative without strategy is called art. Creative with strategy is called advertising.

~ Jeff I. Richards

men between the ages 0f 30 and 50 see the Chiropractor most, then some of the examples you use to describe scenarios in your book should be about what men in that age group are interested in.

Identify your readers/patients' need, even when they don't ask for it. Sometimes, the problem lies unseen; it takes a professional to see it. That professional is you, and through your book, you will be able to address whatever problem they didn't know they had.

An example is the famous Jia Jiang. Jia Jiang did a documentary on how businesses usually say no to unusual requests. To test his assertion, he told a Krispy Kreme outlet to make him a rather unusual request; Olympic-themed donuts. Not only did the store owner make the donuts, he made them with the right colors of the Olympics!

Taking time to listen to people's problems, and then doing more than they requested is a rare skill, and is something your book should be aiming to do; beat expectations and much more. Checking for facts and supporting your ideas with testimonials will create the type of buzz that your readers and patients will talk about and remember.

Don't wait for testimonials too, take an active role in receiving them. Don't expect the testimonials from reading your book to arrive out of the blues. People have jobs and many other things occupying their mind. They might be happy to have bought your book but they probably might not remember to send testimonials. You shouldn't be scared to ask for testimonials. Ask on T.V., ask on radio shows, and ask people when they come for consultations. Ask, ask, and ask. If you wrote a good book, and they've been able to relate to you as people seeking help, they will be willing to give you testimonials.

Also, if you meet people while walking down the streets, or online, and they tell you they loved reading your book and applying all the advice in it, make sure you have record of that. Whether in written form, or in printed format, or text messages, a screenshot; Do whatever is necessary to take

Logic will get you from A to B. Imagination will take you everywhere.

~ Albert Einstein

record of that conversation because they are also testimonials. Through this, you are always reassured that you are on the right path in your career.

After receiving all these testimonials, use them to your advantage. Have them printed and post them on the walls of your office. You can also put them strategically on the home page of your clinic's website. You can also share them on your social media accounts. Keep it in your mind that most readers carry out their own online research before buying books, hence, do not let your website lie fallow. Persuade the readers with testimonials.

So to summarize, just imagine the following scenario......

Imagine a new patient comes into your clinic interested in finding out more about your Stem Cell Therapy Services, and instead of experiencing the typical office visit, imagine the following : Imagine the new patient sits down, and instead of not just getting an intake form to fill out, the patient receives your book, and its not only autographed, but it has a simple but powerful hand written message along the first page of the book that reads: " Dear Mary, may this book inspire you to take your health and your life to the next level, Sincerely, Dr. John."

Now tell me when is the last time a patient experienced this kind of wow factor?

Why It's So Important To Blow Away Your Prospective Patient - Why It's So Critical To Create A Powerful First Impression

In this hyper connected world and large market it is no longer enough to offer a quality product or service. You need to surprise and delight your customers. It is no longer enough to satisfy them. By creating certain benefits, you will create a memorable purchasing experience, strengthen your competitive advantage and boost customer loyalty. As it relates to your profession as a chiropractor, getting your patients to reckon with you

Good ideas come from bad ideas, but only if there are enough of them.

~ Seth Godin

and stay loyal is going to take a lot more than an oily massage of their spines and backs.

A WOW Factor is a commonly use slang term. It is that quality or feature that is *extremely impressive*. Nowadays, we are drawn to people, products and processes that can be described as impressive, engaging, memorable or spectacular. *When people have an intensely positive reaction to something about you or your business, you've got a WOW Factor!*

What do you do to elicit this kind response from your patients? How do you WOW your patients and leave permanent impressions?

1. Innovate. Add an extra feature and/or benefit to the current mode of chiropractic practice. Expand technology. Be the first to market yourself. Become the best. Develop a game-changer. Introduce the next big thing that the practice has never seen before. Differentiate yourself from other competitors. In all you set out to do as a chiropractor, stand out!

2. Become the best deal. Make your spine and back massage services, your customer experience easier, better, faster, or cheaper than your competition. Provide superior quality of service, expertise and professionalism. Offer exceptional value, the most convenient or the best guarantee.

3. Offer overwhelming proof by taking away all doubt about the value of your services as a chiropractor. Include testimonials, outstanding case studies, reviews, demonstrations and samples. Provide statements of authorities, facts or accurate statistics to prove your claims. Nothing is more dumbfounding and awe striking than proof of success. The more interesting, shocking, surprising and compelling your facts and figures are, the greater the WOW Factor. In essence, make your case so convincing that your patients' decisions to keep loyalty with you is not debatable.

Be content to act, and leave the talking to others.

~ Baltasa

4. Impress patients with your exceptional know-how. Knowledge, expertise and professionalism produce immediate confidence with patients. They want to be attended to and given the best of care by those they trust, you, who informs them, educates them, teaches them, and takes them by the hand to show them what to do. In doing so, you take away their worries and frustrations, and make their health burdens lighter.

5. Give terrific customer care. Apply the golden rule (treat customers the way you would like to be treated). Never hesitate to go the extra yard or mile. Exhibit an incomparable degree of integrity. Continually seek for ways to surprise and delight your patients; delight that causes them to return. Better still, delight that causes them to start spreading the word about you and your chiropractic practice.

6. People albeit your patients always will love special treatment. Look for ways in which your chiropractic practice can go that extra mile by doing something rally special for your patients. It doesn't have to cost an arm and a leg nor involve expensive gifts. You could invite your patients to return anytime within a few days of their visit for free touch-up work.

7. Pay attention to the small details. It is often the little details that your patients will remember about your practice; how your staff treated them, the cleanliness of your office and washrooms, the ease of navigation on your website or the simplicity of explanation of certain procedures. Little details such as these are easy to manage and are often inexpensive but can have a huge impact.

8. Remember who your best patients are. With the advent of database creation packages, it has become the more easy to create and keep patient profiles. This way, you can keep track of patient preferences

Your reputation is more important than your paycheck, and your integrity is worth more than your career.

~ Ryan Freitas

or send a card on special occasions. In navigating such option, it is always wise to remember that patient confidentiality and privacy is paramount.

There is always never a second chance to make a first impression. A first impression is an opportunity that never repeats itself. There is a lot to be said about first impressions. First impression are established from the first moments of contact and will dictate the perceived quality of the overall experience to be expected from relating either with you or your book.

If a set of numbers were read out loud, it is arguable but certain that most people would remember the first few numbers and the last few numbers. It's just human nature. It is called the *recency primacy effect*. We tend to remember beginnings and endings. It is the same with patients; they tend to recall what they hear or see at the beginning and the end.

On any given day, you as a chiropractor are probably very busy trying to keep track of the many demands of running your practice and caring for your existing patients. These preoccupations often keep you from putting your best foot forward with new patients.

From the moment you approach a patient and a reader alike, your behaviour, attitude and personal presentation will influence their decisions to relate with you as a patient or as a potential believer and buyer of your authored book. These set of people will make early decisions about you – and how much time they'll give you – based on your appearance, your body language and mannerisms, your tone of voice and facial expressions, your words and your demeanour.

Put yourself in a patient's shoes.

A patient's initial contact with you as a chosen chiropractor often is by phone. If such patient is greeted brusquely or is transferred more than once when just trying to make an appointment, this first impression will be

Chase the vision, not the money, the money will end up following you.

~ Tony Hsieh

negative. Anyone who answers your phones or makes your appointments must be friendly, professional and organized.

Why friendly? Because the chiropractic practice is a caring business. Why professional? Because your staff is an extension of you and your credentials as a chiropractor, and why organized? Because making an appointment should be a straightforward business.

The *second* first impression is the waiting room. This impression occurs when they walk into your office for the first time. It happens in the twinkle of an eye. Very quickly. If your waiting room conveys friendliness, professionalism, organization and neatness, it will be a positive defining moment of truth. Your waiting room or office should be inviting rather than imposing. Patients should feel welcome what with the colours, wall decorations, tables and furniture. Patients are turned off by soiled carpets, faded fabric on mismatched furniture. In the minds of your patient, a dirty waiting room raises concern about the attention to detail of your chiropractic practice. This concern eventually will translate into a questioning of your competencies as a chiropractor. In the same vein, you have to pay attention to your reception area materials as well as signs. Do the majority of your signs pertain to insurance rather than helping the patient feel at ease and comfortable. Any signs that should be put up should be ones that don't add unnecessary tension to what the patient already feels. Instead, they should serve to calm and douse such tensions.

The *third* first impression is in the greetings. Always know that it is in human nature to feel special. Patients are always looking for someone, a chiropractor like you who makes everyone who comes into his waiting room feel like the MVP – most valuable patient. Your greeting either puts a patient at ease or on edge. Your greeting is the best way to create a rapport with your patients. Also realize that going to a doctor may not be everyone's favourite activity and that your patient may be nervous, scared or outright reluctant to see you. Try to put them at ease with your communication styles. Be professional and confident but also

Your work is going to fill a large part of your life, and the only way to be truly satisfied is to do what you believe is great work. And the only way to do great work is to love what you do.

~ Steve Jobs

approachable. Inspiring confidence in your patients is what they have come for. The confidence you display and extend is the perfect key to getting into their minds and establishing a worthy impression of you.

Be the first to always say hello. Don't wait for the patient to speak. Some patients will interpret your reticence as indifference. Use of the patient's name is welcome. Name tags are never a substitute for a personal introduction.

Patient confidentiality is your respect of your patient's privacy. This is another way of creating a first impression. Patients should not have to state the reasons for their visit to your chiropractic practice especially when other people are present. This is why it is always necessary to be prepared for each and every patient. Always review their charts before entering the exam room. Your ability to know and remember information will impress your patients and will also eliminate the need for patients to keep disclosing information they would rather want kept private.

Your appearance shows your patient that you respect them, your chiropractic and/or your book. Respect is one of the attributes that prospective patients and readers of your book look for as value that you are offering. Coming off as disrespectful in every sense of the word is like giving yourself a red card even before a match has started. Nobody wants to have anything to do with someone who is rude and exemplifies rudeness. Be sure your posture is straight, confident and relaxed. Don't distract your patient with personal fidgeting and adjustments or by being distracted while talking or attending to them.

Dress to impress. Nothing can be more disheartening than an unkempt and haggard-looking chiropractor. Long, untidy nails. Unkempt hair. A crooked smile and unclean dentition. Grooming preaches attention to detail. It shows that you care enough for your body and as such will not find it difficult to extend that same care to your patients.

The most dangerous poison is the feeling of achievement. The antidote is to every evening think what can be done better tomorrow.

~ Ingvar Kamprad

Many things affect your chiropractic practice that you have no control over. Your personal attitude, on the other hand, is something that you can control. Your attitude affects the way you approach your patients. Choosing to approach potential patients positively, confidently, enthusiastically, and with a helpful attitude – even in the face of obvious stress or frustration – will improve your credibility and grow your sales. Remember that every business exists to meet the needs of customers. If you believe that your job as a chiropractor is to understand and solve your patients' problems, then you will exude a natural and helpful confidence.

It's not about ideas. It's about making ideas happen.

~ Scott Belsky

CHAPTER 11

HOW WRITING A STEM CELL THERAPY BOOK CREATES THE CELEBRITY STATUS

As a Chiropractor, writing a book is one step closer to being that celebrity that you've always craved. Writing a book confirms you as an expert, and if the book is very good and generates good reviews, you would be a leading expert in chiropractic. You can charge at premium rates for your services, while still getting lots of patients. Your former patients become more loyal than before because you become the real deal after your book's release. They would even refer more patients to your practice.

Here are ways through which a book gives you celebrity status:

a)   Writing a book immediately makes you a popular expert

One of the ways to make yourself a celebrity or a quite popular expert is to write a book. Before anybody picks a book on chiropractic from a bookshelf, they immediately assume the writer is an expert, meaning, you must take advantage of this assumption.

Anna David, New York Times best-selling author of 6 books wrote on how she became an instant celebrity overnight after she wrote her first book "Party girl".

> *"My first book, Party Girl, came out the same year that Lindsay Lohan, Paris Hilton, and Nicole Richie all made headlines for being wild and crazy party girls.*
>
> *Right before the book was released, pretty much out of nowhere, I got a call from The Today Show asking if I would come on and discuss the "party girl*

Don't worry about failure; you only have to be right once.

~ Drew Houston

phenomenon." It was the first time I spoke on TV with the chyron under me that read "Author, Party Girl"—but it wasn't the last.

Even though I had no medical degree, had never worked in a rehab and really knew no more than the average addict who'd been sober for a few years, I had written a book about addiction and so the world believed I knew something about it.

One of the first things I asked my first TV agent when I signed with him was if I should go get a Master's in Psychology so I could have credibility on TV as a so-called expert.

He smiled. "Being on TV," he said, "has given you that credibility."

She was called on to speak on T.V. even when her book was not yet released because they assumed writing a book on addiction made her an expert on such subject matter. Since you have the expertise as a chiropractor, you have a better advantage.

When you decide to write a book, it is important to have a topic in your head that you feel you can talk extensively about. However, as you continue to write, you might realize that you are learning more about other aspects of chiropractic; learning the names of other people who have also done great work in the discipline. You will also learn about new approaches to issues and the different school of thoughts. Hence, writing also presents a rare opportunity for you to do some research career-wise.

b)   Writing a book gives an opportunity for you to sell your work to the press

Writing a book comes with an opportunity to promote yourself. Press conferences, appearances in radio talk shows on chiropractic, TV shows, book signings and author readings at bookstores, etc. Each of these instances gives you opportunities to talk about your practice and your experiences with your patients. You must be ready to say something at every instance. That's the life of a celebrity. Anna David became a regular

Fail often so you can succeed sooner.

~ Tom Kelley

T.V talker and life coach after her first appearance on T.V. because of her book. She was able to sell her work on her first appearance, thereby paving the way for more appearances.

c) Writing a book shows that you know what is the latest trending issue in chiropractic

Writing a book people interested in chiropractic can identify with, surely proves that you know your stuff, and makes it comfortable for them to approach your practice for solutions. Focus on writing a book that is a 'must-have' and not just a 'nice-to-have' book. To grab attention, make sure your book is solving problems in the now; solve needs and not wants.

The foremost search engine in the worlds is google. However, as a writer, you must learn how to use Amazon. It is the foremost search engine for professionals, ranking higher than LinkedIn.

Make sure your book is on Amazon, with an amazing book review. People want to know who wrote books, so be rest assured they will look for the author. Make sure your Amazon profile is up to date. Make sure you are up to date on issues affecting chiropractic.

d) Writing a book keeps you relevant for a long time

When you've written a book, you have an endless amount of content at your disposal to keep you in the public eye for a long time. Whether it's a quote in your book, or a line, or a piece of advice; all these become materials for articles, speeches, blogs, e-books etc. You are never out of the public eye. You can make video messages off your book, create a podcast show, have a T.V segment, be called to speak on the cable network in your area of expertise.

e) Writing a book gives opportunity to give incentives

As mentioned before, people love free things. When you attach a service to the sales of your book, watch the sales profits go high, while you also get

If you're interested in the living heart of what you do, focus on building things rather than talking about them.

~ Ryan Freitas

more patients. Whether in the form of an incentive, where, for instance, you give people who buy your book a free consultation or you give them gift cards, people will buy your books just for this. Your reputation will soar.

f) Writing a book opens the door to speaking opportunities

It is really amazing how you quickly become a keynote speaker at conferences when you write a book on chiropractic. Whether it's a seminar or a workshop, getting to be chosen as a speaker in these events is difficult, except you have authored a book talking about chiropractic.

When you want to speak at a conference, do you send online links or business cards to the conference organizers? Or a book? Make sure you send a book. Being a writer ensures that you get better speaking opportunities and invites. If your book doesn't add more to the body of knowledge on chiropractic, then it is a waste of time.

Whenever the media needs an expert opinion, they approach an expert. How do they recognize an expert? The expert's book. A book is the first real proof of authority. It proves that you know what you're talking about.

If you want to be seen in your field so as to gain media coverage, write a book that proves you are an expert, and the media coverage will come for you. They want to hear from experts, and the expertise of the author is their judgement of the book. Most times, it's a cyclical event. The media invites you to talk; then you speak extensively about your vocation and your book, causing listeners to buy your book so that they will learn more about you and your practice. This will then lead to other media engagements because now, everyone wants to hear you speak.

g) Writing a book helps to focus your message and make you unique i.e. different from your closest competitor.

Before you write a book on 'Spinal manipulation for low back pain', you must make sure no one else has anything on that. Or you might just be

Entrepreneur is someone who has a vision for something and a want to create.

~ David Karp

repeating what has already been said. You need to carve a niche for yourself as a chiropractic author, so when someone who's read your book wants to recommend you to another person, they would know you are the only authority, or the first, in that area.

Writing a book helps to provide a clue to the core principles of your chiropractic practice, and helps potential patients understand what you are really all about. It also makes the core values of your business clearer to the people who work for you.

Many people have gotten lots of attention because they wrote a book. Even when you felt you knew more than them, they got their knowledge and expertise verified simply because people read their book. This is why it is better to write about a particular topic, rather than the whole broad chiropractic practice; it helps you make your money quicker. You are able to stand out and create a brand for yourself faster.

In 2006, Mike Schulz, principal of the Wellesley Hills Group, in Framingham, Massachusetts, decided to research how writing a book helps your business, and the results were released through a book titled 'The Business Impact of Writing a Book.'

He said this about their findings:

> *"We found out that people who self-published, didn't use a literary agent or hire a PR firm, and didn't do a lot of public speaking, sold fewer books and were much less pleased with the process...The vast majority of the authors we surveyed -- 96% -- said they did realize a significant positive impact on their businesses from writing a book and would recommend the practice."*

The last 10% it takes to launch something takes as much energy as the first 90%.

~ Rob Kalin

CHAPTER 12

HOW WRITING A STEM CELL THERAPY BOOK CREATES THE GURU EFFECT

Using your knowledge of your chiropractic practice should be the first thing you think about when you want to sell yourself to people. To be considered a guru, a go-to expert in your field, you need to create a niche for yourself where people can see the wealth of knowledge you have regarding an issue. The best kind of place to create that space is to author a book.

Writing a book gives you a platform to change perceptions and dogmas. Books should be written in such a way as to change people's perception of things, and when they are written that way, the author will never be forgotten.

Ryan had a Chiropractic practice, with a lot of patients, and was well known by both colleagues and competitors. Everybody knew he was the guru of Chiropractic, the teacher. However, when the media needed someone to give a comment to the public on chiropractic issues, they called on people who had written a book on chiropractic. At that moment, Ryan knew he had to write a book. Though he knew he was an expert, he wondered how he was going to write chiropractic in a way that people would learn from his book.

For many people like Ryan, writing a book is a daunting task. However, remember, you are not the only voice in your field. Someone else is planning to write a book on chiropractic too, probably in the same aspect, you want to write about. You can't afford to be relaxed about it. It's a race against time.

Ideas are easy. Implementation is hard.

~ Guy Kawasaki

Before you put pen to paper to write a book about chiropractic, you have to first consider many things; especially if you want the book to project you as a guru in your field.

1. Know what you want to write about

When I say 'know', I don't mean you should question what you already know. Be sure of what you want to write about particularly. Too many people, after they've decided to write, sit down and just begin to write. At the end of the day, they are rejected by publishers because their writing has no focus and no authority on any subject. Relax and ask yourself these questions before you write: What do I hope to achieve with this book? Who are the particular people that need to read this book? What are chiropractors looking for that would make them buy my book?

If you are able to answer these questions very well, while also aligning them with your wealth of knowledge, then you are ready to begin writing.

2. Outline what you want to teach your readers

Imagine you are sitting in front of your patients, and they tell you a problem they are facing. Imagine again that the problem is exactly what you are addressing in your book. Now, write down exactly the answers you would give the patient, taking it step by step, for the benefit of your readers. By the time you finish doing this, you would have successfully outlined the purpose of your book effectively. You would have provided clarity just as if you were a teacher explaining concepts to students.

3. Talk it out with someone

After you have successfully outlined your points in your head and on a rough paper somewhere, you need to be interviewed by someone close to you, so you can expatiate on the key points in your book. Get a recording device, have someone ask you questions about your book while recording the conversation, and you would realize that you would get more talking

Timing, perseverance, and ten years of trying will eventually make you look like an overnight success.

~ Biz Stone

points for your book, even better than if you had gone straight to writing from your detailed outlining.

4. Transcribe the interview

The next thing to do is to get everything said in that interview written on paper. What you would have done is that you would have covered every ground regarding your book. The beautiful part is they are your words all written down; the ugly part is you need to edit and make them beautiful to the eyes. They would be horribly written; a transcript of jumbled together ideas. Sit down and sort through them, imagining yourself teaching a class.

Editing your work can be tedious. You could either give a professional editor or you do the work yourself. You have to look at your work with a keen eye, analyzing your own work closely. It can drain you, but knowing how hard it was for you to put every single word on that page, you know it is worth it.

Joe Baldwin, CEO OF Essaylook had this to say about the writing process.

> *"By taking a critical look at your own work, that you care so much about, you'll learn valuable skills in how to critique a piece without insulting the creator...these skills will make you a better manager of others — by spending time in their shoes, you'll be better equipped to offer guidance, instead of condescension."*

After you have edited your book, then you are ready to publish.

There are some skills writing a book unearths in you, skills you don't know you had.

The first is Time management. Like it was said before, writing a book can be a daunting task. When you decide to be an author, you have to get better with managing your time, and with finding the motivation to write, because these skills will be needed on short notice to get you through the writing process.

When I'm old and dying, I plan to look back on my life and say 'wow, that was an adventure,' not 'wow, I sure felt safe.

~ Tom Preston-Werner

It's easy to get distracted today, with the advent of social media and sensational news. You just need to keep focus, using the steps listed above. Learning to keep your mind amidst different distractions is the true hallmark of a guru.

To be a guru in anything is to be an authority in that subject matter. Writing a book makes you an authority.

The word authority begins with author, meaning that, as the latter, you have instant respect and

Your book gives you instant authority, even in no way your numerous tweets or Facebook posts would give you.

Sonia Simone, the co-founder of Copyblogger Media has given a few tips on what it means to be an authority on a subject. She broke it into five parts:

1) *Authorities serve their audiences. Zig Ziglar said, "You will get all you want in life if you help enough other people get what they want."*

2) *Authorities genuinely know their stuff. There's a lot of junk out there. If you can provide beneficial information which is easily accessible, you will have authority.*

3) *Authorities care. People instinctively know when you care. There's no gaming this process.*

4) *Authorities are strategic. Show how your expertise and authority can help others translate their effort into building their business.*

5) *Authorities take the long view. Shortcuts take far too long. The long game generates success.*

Anything that is measured and watched, improves.

~ Bob Parsons

CHAPTER 13

HOW WRITING A BOOK ON STEM CELL THERAPY GIVES YOU THE ULTIMATE LEVERAGE TO EDUCATE YOUR PATIENTS ON WHAT YOU DO

Writing a book is beyond gaining attention though. Advertisements get people's attention, but they don't tell them how to make a decision regarding the products being advertised. We now know where people look for information about a product; they listen to their friends and family, they listen to radio talk shows, they watch television programs, they google the internet, and they read books.

However, when they are not satisfied with all of these interactions, and they want more, and where do they find that more? They look for the mailing address of that talk show guest, they search for information on Wikipedia, and they look for the address of the author of that book. They search for the person who practically wrote the book on the topic they want to understand clearly.

Erika Anderson, a Forbes contributor says writing a book is good business because it gives your business credibility.

> *"If you're running a business and you publish a good book, your business gets a halo effect from your rise in credibility. Being associated with a book and its author gives an enterprise legitimacy in the eyes of the world. Being considered more legitimate simply makes it easier to get things done. In my experience, it also gives a lift to everyone who works in the organization - it becomes a source of pride and esprit de corps."*

See things in the present, even if they are in the future.

~ Larry Ellison

Writing a book brings people to you, lets people know exactly how good you are, and proves to them that you can be of help to them. It's the best tool at your disposal for building your practice and getting more patients.

People wouldn't probably listen to you if you gave them a sales pitch of how you are a good chiropractor. They would want to see proof, and that can only happen when you walk the talk, as written in your book.

If you own a clinic, and you have also spent time and money building an online presence, probably through having a website or a blog, your book on your website could be that missing piece to you having more visitors on your website, and more patients in your clinic. You can also use your book as a pitch for a conference you've been hoping to speak at for a very long time. They say time is money, and many business owners today don't seem to have that luxury. Your book will represent you in places where you can't go. Most businesses are calling the process of writing a book 'A Master's degree' because it's like that extra qualification that might just earn you a place at the table of 'big boys.'

The owner of a consulting agency had this to say about writing a book as a business owner:

> *"One of our clients spent 15 years rising to the top of the employee rewards space. Today, he boasts dozens of Fortune 500 companies as clients. He recently launched a book that explains how he built a dynamic company by rewarding his employees. He then sent a copy of his new book to every one of his clients. The book has brought even more clients through the door."*

Data published by Next Century Publishing revealed that business owners who have authored a book on their businesses are twice as likely to win new business. For chiropractors, it means if you write a book, your chances of getting new patients to register in your clinic are doubled.

If you intend on writing a book, make sure you do it right. Do not rush the process because you want to 'get something out there'. Over the years,

Opportunities don't happen. You create them.

~ Chris Grosser

since the advent of e-books, there have been thousands of PDF file books transferred all over the internet. Without having a way for tracking the number of people who downloaded the books, because most of them are free, these authors call themselves 'best-selling' authors. However, they are never called to speak on the topic matters as experts, because, let's face it, free e-books are not real books.

If you want to write, then do it the right way. Write a book, publish it with a good publisher, and you are on your way to becoming an author. By doing so, you will be building your personal brand, establishing your competence and will be doing more than if you just wrote periodical articles.

As you write your book, you must create a picture of the type of audience you are targeting. You begin to add angles, nuances, more details, a certain level of grammar, vocabulary etc. as you continue to write. At the end of the day, you will start to realize that your book is targeted towards a specific kind of demographics. That realization makes you identify your real audience, the kind of people you are targeting with your book.

This also helps you to go back to work with a better plan of how you're going to take your practice to your target audience. You also have an idea on how to get your messages to them.

Ideas are commodity. Execution of them is not.

~ Michael Dell

CHAPTER 14

HOW WRITING A BOOK ON STEM CELL THERAPY ALLOWS YOU TO CHARGE PREMIUM PRICES FOR YOUR SERVICES

Writing a book will bring attention to your practice but that's not all it can bring for you. It can also bring money. You should be able to turn all that attention your book gives you into money. Your book's success allows you to charge premium prices for your services, including with the new patients.

Services to be offered could include consultations, coaching etc. You might think you've written all you can write in the book, and no one would pay you for consultation. However, the opposite is the truth. Your book puts you on the map, makes you important and gives you authority to talk about chiropractic. People will not then be paying for your wisdom as shown in your book, though it's part of the bargain. What they will be paying for is your authority as an expert chiropractor.

Melissa Gonzalez, the writer of *Pop Up Paradigm: How Brands build Human Connections in a Digital Age,* a book about Pop-Up retail, says she has made more than a million dollars from the book. She did that by selling less than 1000 copies of the book. When she was asked why she wrote her book, she had this to say:

"Did it become a bestseller? No."

"Did I think that was going to happen? No."

"Did I write it because I thought book sales were going to be my new bread and butter? No."

I knew that if I failed I wouldn't regret that, but I knew the one thing I might regret is not trying.

~ Jeff Bezos

'Those are extra to me. I really wrote it to grow the business and the investment paid for itself."

She wrote her book to promote her business, and not to really sell copies.

Now, she is one of the world's most important expert on pop-up retail. Many people don't care, or don't know about retail, talk less about buying books on retail. However, she had a target audience for her book.

Her target audience was the top executives in retail, the kind of people that would hire her as a consultant. She captured their attention by listing in her book the different methods she created in pop-up retail. These methods were used by her to resuscitate floundering businesses in retail. Her book had the attention it got, though it didn't make many sales because she was the first person to talk extensively about that aspect of retail. Hence, because of this, she became a leading voice in that field of retail.

This led to the desired effect she wanted, the real reason why she wrote a book in the first place; everyone came to her for advice on pop up retail, especially the top executives.

It was at this point she began to charge premium prices for her services. Her consulting business took off; she signed a multi-million dollar contract with one of America's largest mall companies to help a new retail plan. Her book took her to where she couldn't go before. It got her the attention she needed and her business took off from there.

That's the point. People who hire consultants and coaches are hiring them to teach them and their team and to implement their knowledge. They're often not looking to learn the knowledge in the book. The book is how you show them that they should hire you.

Writing a book is becoming a fad now, and has been called the new master's Degree. There's a reason every expert and authority on a particular subject matter is being known as thought leaders now. They have all written good books that people in their field have acknowledged as some

If you are not embarrassed by the first version of your product, you've launched too late.

~ Reid Hoffman

kind of manual. Most thought leaders are now consultants with consultant firms on the side. Think John Maxwell, Robert Kiyosaki, John Hagel etc.

As you consider writing a book, you might be thinking 'where is the logic in hiring, as a consultant, someone who wrote a book where he talked about what he knows?'

That is exactly why you need to write. You will not be hired to consult for what is in the book; you will be hired for what is in your head, to teach them and their team. The book is your business pitch; why they should hire you.

Here are ways through which you can make more money when you write a book.

Be an evolutionary speaker

The major way to make money from your book is to speak on it; become a speaker. And if you are already a speaker, this is the opportunity to raise the price of your expertise. Without writing a book, it will be very hard to be paid highly for speaking gigs. People have speaking careers without books, but they eventually had to write a book. They also usually charge higher for their services after they've written a book.

Your book is your new business card; it speaks for you in boardrooms. It is the way company executives know you are qualified to talk to them about a particular topic.

Kevin Kruse is an example of thought leaders who had regular speaking gigs before they ever wrote a book. He is a public speaker, an entrepreneur, and now an author. In his blog Author Journey to 100k, he mentioned that he made a lot of money in his first year as a writer; earning $70,000 in book sales. However, his speaking fees soared up higher; he made $170,000.

All humans are entrepreneurs not because they should start companies but because the will to create is encoded in human DNA.

~ Reid Hoffman

Leverage on your book content; be creative

You can also leverage your book by creating a video course or a podcast series based on the lessons in the book, in a way that you will make more money from the book.

If your book has lessons for readers, especially when the application of those lessons creates many returns for them that testimonials begin to pour in, then you need to leverage on this. Create an advanced version of it either in the form of a video course or a podcast series and charge for more.

It has been discovered that, while people might not pay to buy a book for more than $25, they eventually pay more for videos or podcasts. In fact, they pay more than 100 times more for them.

This is logical, because people have different learning styles, and the most popular learning style is the video and the audio. Books come least as a preferred style of learning.

However, the most important point is, writing a book, and looking for other ways to sell material on it is a great way to command premium prices for your services.

Teach professional workshops at big companies

You can also get paid for workshops. Sometimes, workshops are combined with speaking gigs. However, they are not the same thing.

Many present-day consultants now conduct workshops for businesses. You are brought in to teach your methods, listed in your books, to employees, and you are to train them for days, up to a week most times. Many of the companies who do this are large companies, who have to conduct training classes intermittently for their employees. They hire experts and thought

In the end, a vision without the ability to execute it is probably a hallucination.

Steve Case

leaders, especially authors, to hold seminars and workshops inside company buildings for the employees. These big companies usually pay a lot, even for one-day workshops.

Workshops are essentially important because most people know they don't really create time to read through all of a book. Many employers know if they ask their employees to read a book, they probably aren't going to read it. However, if they get the writer of the book to come to the office building to talk, and give lessons, and to answer questions, many employees would create time for it.

You can still make money from book sales

Now, talking about book sales itself; you can make money from book sales. Though it is not the best way to make money, you can still make money from it. Why would you go through the effort of writing a book, and not expect to make anything from the book?

The problem with focusing on book sales alone is it might mess up with the writing process. It could cause some agitation in the writer, an anxiety to impress to the extent that they might get a writer's block. Just focus on everything as a whole; the book sales, marketing, the other gigs etc.

When you know your book appeals to a particular audience, there are many ways you can sell to them:

1. You can set up ads on Facebook. Facebook ads for books often generate sales.

2. You can set up a promotion campaign, where you give people free things as an incentive for them to buy your book. In your case as a chiropractor, you can offer a free consultation.

3. You will also have the opportunity to sell your books at events, especially when you are a speaker at the event. Many people buy

147

Don't be cocky. Don't be flashy. There's always someone better than you.

~ Tony Hsieh

4. books like this; when they go to events and listen to a speaker for the first time. If the speaker does well, the listeners are usually not satisfied with what they've heard, they usually want more, and so they end up buying the books.

5. You can apply to be featured in someone's column on a newspaper or blog, and share the lessons from your book in those columns. This usually has the effect of the readers wanting more; leading to more book sales.

However, if you've positioned yourself and your book with the points listed in referral marketing, and holding workshops etc., book sales wouldn't really matter.

Embrace what you don't know, especially in the beginning, because what you don't know can become your greatest asset. It ensures that you will absolutely be doing things different from everybody else.

~ Sara Blakely

CHAPTER 15

THE IMPORTANCE OF MARKETING – HOW MARKETING IS EVERYTHING

How would you describe the 'fruits of your labour'? How would you describe boycotting an important meeting you have planned with sweat and blood? Would you spend hours sitting behind a notebook studying for an exam and not eventually write it? Enjoying the fruits of your labour means that you would not deliberately do these things.

The fruits of your labour are the rewards you get from expending resources. They are the respite you get from slaving away. They are the sweet sighs you let out when all's been said and done. The fruits of your labour are the satisfaction you get from doing something worthwhile and fulfilling.

As a chiropractor, the fruits of your labour are the smiles you get when you walk down hospital corridors and get a hundred thumbs-ups. They are the approval nods you get from patients whose backs and spines you have healed. More importantly, as a chiropractor-author, the fruits of your labour aren't the millions of book copies still sitting on dusty shelves. They are the books that have managed to find themselves on the shelves of the larger population.

Despite the obvious and increasing connectedness of everything, and the consequential increase in demand for practically everything, there are still plenty of stuff that don't get to see the light. Many authors still think that writing a book ends at the last full stop. They think that news of their book's publication will magically be translated and transcribed onto the minds of the population.

"Make your customer the hero of your stories."

~ Ann Handley

If as a chiropractor, you are thinking about promoting your book(s), then there really is just one question to be asked: how will anyone know my book exists if I don't literally shout it out loud from the rooftops? How will anyone know my book exists if I don't go all out to make sure that the songs on peoples' lips are borne from the lyrics of my book?

And that's all any good marketing is all about! The ability to engage the population with the stories that you have to tell, the experiences that you have to share, which will so much inspire them to buy a copy and also tell their friends and family about it, allowing the quality to do the speaking.

The most important aspect of the publishing world is the marketability of work done.

Many new authors overlook the importance of author publicity. Instead, they want to stay in the shadows and push their book to the light. But it rarely works that way. Books can generate more sales *if the reader(s) can associate it with the author.*

What makes your book about chiropractic better than the one with whom it shares a cataloguing number? If readers can positively associate you, as a chiropractor, with your book, then, there's a better chance that they will pick it up instead of a counterpart.

Let's look at the importance of branding as one of the teeth to drive the gear of marketing.

The objectives of a good brand is to deliver your message clearly, connect emotionally with your target audience and eventually motivate the buyer(s) to buy. Ultimately, the aim is to establish and make concrete their loyalty.

As it relates to authors, especially a chiropractor-authors, we sometimes feel that our books will just sell. But, let's think realistically. How many times have you purchased a product that hadn't been *consistently marketed* to you? Emphasis on the italicized. How many times have you opted to pay for something that has not had ample publicity that appeals to you? The

"Marketing is too important to be left to the marketing department."

~ David Packar

answer is probably none. This is because as humans, we tend to naturally gravitate towards that which has been imprinted on our psyche. This is what marketing does – weigh heavy on your mind (emotionally) until you translate such emotions into eventual willingness and ability to purchase.

An illustration.

Joseph sells his product on streets, alleyways and bus stops. For a ridiculously low amount, say $4, he offers these products for sale yet people reluctantly and most often decline to buy. Why? Because they've never heard of him! They don't know what the quality of the product is. They don't know if Joseph is any good at what he does. The list of uncertainties goes on and on.

Now, put Joseph on a social site, let's say Facebook. He's consistently posting new goods and services. He's posting descriptions and updates. He's backing his claims up with pictures and videos. You find out eventually that the products are of good quality judging by the testimonials and comments you see and scroll through. Later, he posts that he's offering such product for same $4. Now, you've gotten to know him better. You have an idea of his product quality and you understand his passion. You may or may not buy eventually, but the chances are better that you will because you've connected with him.

What has just been described is branding.

Your audience want to know YOU as an author, especially as an author of a not-too-frequently-written-about field and genre as chiropractic. A catchy title and a nice cover alone will not be the only thing to persuade someone to buy your book, especially in a plethora of books.

Marketing your book is about leveraging your own personal backstory. In this fast-paced world, information is in abundance so much so that it continually washes over us. Yet still, only a few things stick. The messages

"Don't find customers for your products, find products for your customers."

~ Seth Godin

we do remember are generally connected to stories. And the key to any good story is *relatability*.

So, what's your story? As a chiropractor, what is that story that endears you to your patients and vice versa? What is that story that is sure to arrest the emotions of those who hear and read about it? What is that story that bears the marks of originality? Find that story, weave it into every press release and presentation, and selling it will be no issue. Marketing is all about leveraging your uniqueness as a chiropractor-author. Your book is merely your calling card to gain entry to bigger things.

We've continually made mention of 'competition'. This refers to other books out there. But in the real sense, according to Hugh Howey, 'writers are not in competition with each other, but with everything else that begs for a reader's attention' like television, social media, etc.

Developing a marketing plan and audience platform will not happen overnight. It is essential that you have a marketing plan for your book. This plan should include research on who will buy your book (your target market) and research into what influences them. Doing this will help you concentrate on the key areas and focus your energy where it's needed. For example, there's no point in concentrating and focusing all attention and marketing efforts to an uneducated community since your book dwells more on chiropractic.

Re-Framing Your Marketing Beliefs

Some authors think that marketing oneself is akin to forcing yourself on people. This is simply no truth. As an author who is coming from a background as a chiropractor, there is always the need to re-frame certain marketing thoughts that have been built up overtime. Certain myths and untrue tales.

"Business has only two functions – marketing and innovation."

~ Peter Drucker

Marketing in a comic and serious sense is akin to sharing something you love and feel passionate about with like-minded people – your patients and readers alike. The catch is finding this target audience, your readers.

In essence, we all are sales persons, whether we are selling the concept of saving to our children, selling ourselves and competencies to our bosses to clinch a promotion or raise, pitching our book to agents or publishers as authors, or getting people to be interested in what we have written. At every stage of your book's progress, marketing is very important; when it launches, after launch and during building long term audiences.

Marketing Your Book When It Launches

From earlier chapters, it has been stated and affirmed that the best plan is one that is executed on time and considering prevailing factors. Launching your book as an author is the first major step to getting the much needed sales and exposure. Getting the word out is the first and major hurdle to scale.

Without adequate marketing, people can't even know about your book, and if they don't know about your book, they obviously can't buy it! Secondly, people see hundreds of ads for many different books. The truth is that the book market is saturated with all books competing for the same audience as yours. If you want to get the needed attention, all you have to do is be unique, different and better than all of your competitor authors. Different and better!

1. Book reviews are a helpful way in positioning your book online. Reviewers are always on hand to provide the best of candid reviews that will eventually drive your sales. By sending free books to these set of people who work in the genre of chiropractic and/or related health genres, you ensure that you get the best of reviews, whether positive or otherwise. Book reviews are the ultimate word of mouth.

"Marketing takes a day to learn and a lifetime to master."

~ Phil Kolter

A vast majority of readers seek recommendations when making a book purchase of any kind. The more reviews you are able to garner as an author, the stronger you are represented. This translates to exposure to more buyers. At the end of the day, each additional review you bag bolsters your chances of catching the eye of another potential buyer.

There is no such thing as 'too many reviews' unless you wold also like to believe that there is such a thing as 'too many sales'.

2. For a brand as yours to be successful, it needs to market itself and do it very well. A cliché? Yes. Traditional media has always been at the forefront of book marketing and advertising, dominating for ages. While it seems that the new media is gaining more grounds, it doesn't for one render traditional advertising obsolete. The traditional media comprises of television, radio, newspaper, direct mail, magazine, outdoor/billboard advertising, yellow pages and print. Being on TV or any of these other channels does not necessarily translate to sales of your book.

Traditional media have a widespread, yet targeted reach. Traditional news outlets have spent years cultivating readers, listeners and viewers, and they are gurus when it comes to reaching targeted audience segments. They remain a trusted source of information. When it comes to news, there is no substitute for a factual story. New media deliver information in headlines and sound bites. Traditional media provide a deeper depth into stories.

However, consider how many books that you as a person has purchased by mere hearing the author speak. The trick here is to target media outlets that align with chiropractic and/or other related field, as well as with your topic, and really personalize the message in terms of what their audiences stand to get from listening to or hearing from you.

3. Your book is actual solid evidence of your experience cum your writing efforts. It's time to let the avid readers out there know that there is something that has been brewing, something new to add to

"Good content isn't about good storytelling. It's about telling a true story well."

~ Ann Handley

their libraries. One of the best marketing techniques is to host a book launch event. A book launch is any form of activity that is created to promote the release of a book. The way books are purchased has changed dramatically over the centuries. Everybody generally will resonate with the idea of throwing a party to celebrate your newly published book on chiropractic.

Conversely, a book tour is another form of book launch. Writing is an art form that is universally appreciated. Touring ensures worldwide exposure for your book (as well as for yourself). Plus, there's a chance that you get to publish your book in multiple, appealing languages.

Reading sessions are another form of book launch. This involves approaching potential venues like bookstores, libraries, and places of worship, parks, schools and the likes. Organizing reading sessions invite the chance of a very personal and intimate moment between you and your readers. By so doing, you build a loyal fan base.

4. Paid advertising is another way to market your book. This is simple. Several social media sites like Facebook offer access to paid advertising where prospective buyers can be directed to a page where they can buy your book.

5. A website is one of the surest ways of gaining and amassing popularity for your book. This is coming from the fact that the internet is the reigning thing when it comes to reaching a broader audience. At every point in time, someone somewhere is on a phone or computer trying to access one information or the other. What better way to get your book out there than launching a website. This will involve you registering a domain name and URL, either under your name (as a chiropractor/author) or for the title of your book. This will make your book available in the vast ocean of online materials and with the right strategies and plans, your book is well on its way to being scrolled to and eventually purchased.

"You can never go wrong by investing in communities and the human beings within them."

~ Pam Moore

6. Blogging is a great way to build attention and engage with your audience over time. A blog is a series of informative posts which relate to your main topics on chiropractic and chiropractic practices. A blog could be set up independently or incorporated into your website, all to attract an audience to your content.

7. List building and email marketing involves creating forms on your website to collect peoples' mail addresses, mainly to keep them updated about your book and other promotional content. You could also include a sign-up link which will help you inform your readers of future books, should you choose to write them. You can also send out newsletters and links to your blogs.

8. The social media channels available today make it more imperative, the need to go global, leveraging on the numerous capabilities that these channels seek to offer. Based on your genre as chiropractic, you can connect with people on Facebook, Twitter, Instagram, LinkedIn, YouTube and many others.

9. Networking is a great way to let people know about your upcoming or already published book. Networking should be done with like-minded people who will help build an excitement around your book or launch. Social networking is about connecting with people. Focus on building relationships with people. Behind every profile is a person. Over time, these people could become fans and advocates of you and your work.

Another less charted course is the way of merchandizing. Merchandizing most often is done after a book has become highly rated and popular. Still, it can be done on a smaller scale, before it gets popular. Printing your character or certain salient dialogues and quotes from your book on T-shirts, mugs, wallpapers, face caps and various items is a sure way of getting the much needed attention from prospective readers and the general population alike.

"Our jobs as marketers are to understand how the customer wants to buy and help them to do so."

~ Bryan Eisenberg

Marketing is like riding a bicycle. The moment you stop pedalling and stop moving, you fall. In other words, marketing never ends. You as a chiropractor-author should and must be eager to market and sell your book. This eagerness and love should be strong even more than the desire to write the book. Remember, if you don't provide value, marketing will probably do more harm than good to you.

"Marketing is really just about sharing your passion."

~ Michael Hyatt

CHAPTER 16

IMPORTANCE OF CREATING A UNIQUE COMPETITIVE ADVANTAGE (UNIQUE SELLING PROPOSITION)

Why Are You The Obvious Choice For Your Prospective Client?

In the words of Charles de Lint, 'no one else sees the world the way you do, so no one else can tell the stories that you have to tell'.

Yes, this holds true almost all the time. Nobody sees the chiropractic profession the way you do. Nobody knows the world of your patients than you do. Nobody can capture the emotions of your patients and clients more than you do. But does this mean that readers will choose to read your book over thousands of others? Does this automatically translate to people resonating with the contents of your work than with others in the same profession or genre? Unfortunately no.

The book market is an obviously crowded place, full of authors all trying to catch the attention of the same set of people you are trying to impress – readers. The internet, TV, radio and print media are all agog with pleas and urges to readers to give some book a try. This noise is deafening? Amidst all this hype is you and your (little) book on chiropractic. It seems as if you're eventually going to drown in this sea of bestsellers.

How then do you break through this noise?

Before you can begin to sell your book to anyone else, you have to sell yourself on it. The easiest way is by defining a specific, unique selling

What do you need to start a business? Three simple things: know your product better than anyone. Know your customer, and have a burning desire to succeed.

~ Dave Thomas

proposition (USP) for your book. This phrase was coined in the 1940s by ad execs. This USP is the best link between your book, your audience and the market. It is typically a short statement that succinctly conveys why your readers should purchase. In other words, why should anyone buy your book(s)? What benefit does your book offer to readers that cannot be found anywhere else? If you walked into a bookstore and there were only three similar books, all by different authors, sitting next to each other on shelf, what would make a potential buyer reach to pick your book first? Unless you can pinpoint what makes your book unique, you cannot target your sales efforts successfully. No matter what industry you are in albeit the writing industry, it is possible to create something that sets you apart.

Many businesses albeit book authors make the mistake of standing for everything when they first start out. They want to do everything well, and they want to be all things to people. They want to be known for having the best quality book contents AND the lowest cost prices. They want to have the best chiropractic practice AND the cheapest costs for patients. They want to be known for practically everything. The problem is this; *when you make attempts to be known for everything, you eventually don't become known for anything.* A remake of the popular jack of all trades.

Advantages of a well-crafted USP include clear differentiation, improved revenue, loyal reading audience and simpler selling of you as a chiropractor and as an author, your book.

Differentiation as far as being a chiropractor-author is concerned, is your book attribute that separates you from competitors. A USP makes your differences clear to your prospects and compels them to strongly consider you. Without a USP, you allow the prospect's buying decision to become vague. These attributes – unique features, quality materials, better writing style(s) as well as brand reputation – help you create a unique USP.

When you offer a USP and your prospects clearly see it, your revenue typically improves or exceeds expectations. It is a true and general notion that people only buy books that best matches their needs, and that offers

171

Whether you think you can, or think you can't – you're right.

~ Henry Ford

the best combination of benefits and price. Most people don't actually know why they need the things they want. Why? Because our decision-making processes as humans don't exactly follow a rule book. Once you realize how your readers make purchases, especially book purchases, and understand what your greatest USP is, you'll have a streamlined marketing strategy with focused goals.

The truth is that without a USP, you will struggle to form an identity

The best way to understanding your audience buying process is to put yourself in their shoes. Too often, authors fall too much in love with their books that they sometimes forget that it is the readers' needs, not their own, that they seek to and must satisfy. Readers make decisions based on logical factors before they opt to buy your new book. And each one of these steps need to be understood and/or acknowledged before you pick up your USP. Knowing what motivates your readers' behaviour and buying decisions requires you to fill in the shoes of an amateur psychologist. These phases are what every reader goes through in the process of buying a book albeit your book;

1. The reader identifies and recognizes a need in his life that can be provided for by a product – a book

2. Subsequently, he (will) searches for any information about the book that will stand to fulfil his aching needs

3. He then evaluates this book based on its features. This evaluation is done according to his requirements and preferences

4. The reader now wants to consider his options before he makes the purchase. This he does in terms of alternative products that are available; how differently they are priced, where they are readily available as well as the most convenient way to acquire them. The reader then makes his purchase

Behold the turtle, he makes progress only when he sticks his neck out.

~ Bruce Levin

5. The reader then uses the book purchased and formulates an opinion about the book/author brand and the book itself

6. The reader then disposes of the book (or not) and perhaps replaces it with a better alternative.

The key to understanding and crafting a worthy USP is basically to earn *reader loyalty*. Reader loyalty is described in terms of readers who buy your books instead of others at every given opportunity, who recommend them to their friends, and are more than willing to pay a little more to get quality from a chiropractor-author. Such loyalty could be behavioural in the sense that the reader buys your book(s) regularly and does not respond to competitors' offerings, or attitudinal, wherein a reader buys with respect to the degree to which he prefers your brand and book.

In order to have an effective USP, you must make sure that your advertisements make a proposition to your patients and readers that your competitor cannot. Why spend months or even years acquiring knowledge and eventually crafting a book that may end up being buried by similar work?

It's vital to get things right as it relates to your USP. Readers cannot keep re-evaluating books every time they need to make purchases. To make life easier for themselves, they tend to organize books into groups and position them accordingly – for instance, the best motivational book, the most explanatory book, and the best value book.

What is a competitive advantage? You should be able to pull out of a hat, one or two things that you believe you are good at, that your book seeks to explore. Make a list of your competitors – peer chiropractors, fellow authors or even fellow chiropractor-authors – and see what needs they are meeting. Evaluate how well they meet those needs on a scale of say one to five (1 – 5). Just because an author currently has a good position in the market doesn't mean that he is delivering on it! If there's a way you can do it better, then, that's a string basis for market entry and eventual takeover.

Fearlessness is like a muscle. I know from my own life that the more I exercise it the more natural it becomes to not let my fears run me.

~ Arianna Huffington

At the same time, you need to look at those needs of readers that aren't being met. Trends in the writing industry. Trends in the chiropractic industry. Consider those current trends and associated issues that will be most important in the nearest future. Extend your advantage into these areas. Your USP is a strong statement that drives the development of you and your brand as a chiropractor and an author.

How then do you craft a specialized USP as a chiropractor cum author?

1. Have an **honest** conversation with staff (if you have), especially those who have direct contact with your patients, clients and readers. Once you have gathered these individuals, have a brainstorming session and answer these questions;
    *   Why is our chiropractic practice or our book a 'must have'?
    *   What are the advantages and benefits of choosing us over the competition?

Note down everything that will be said. Some would sound pleasing to the ears, others not. In all, everything said is productive because you need to know not only what you want your USP to be, but also how you are currently perceived in the eyes of the public. A dose of reality is needful once in a while. You also may discover benefits to your brand that you hadn't considered before.

2. Find out if you're unique by going through the list you made above. Cross out anything that your competitors can also claim. Is there anything left?
3. Brainstorm possible benefits of your USP. Answer these questions;
    *   What void in the book market can you fill?
    *   What stands as an utmost guarantee about your service as a chiropractor or about your book as an author?
    *   What is 'bad' about the non-fiction writing industry that a large population loathe?

Risk more than others think is safe. Dream more than others think is practical.

~ Howard Schultz

The major key here is to understand what causes heartache in the chiropractic practice industry as well as in the non-fiction writing industry. Things your patients and clients alike hate.

In the long run, you might have to make reasonable but needed changes to your brand so as to create something that is truly unique to you. Every good product solves a problem. Can you think of a problem that your book solves? Do this and crafting a USP will be the easiest thing to do and you are well on your way to edging out your competitors by cementing a permanent spot in the hearts and minds of your readers.

Diligence is the mother of good luck.

~ Benjamin Franklin

CHAPTER 17

ELEVATING YOUR SELF-CONCEPT AND ITS IMPACT ON SELF-ESTEEM AND SELF-WORTH

The larger part of this text is centred on attaining the power of authority, how to use your book as a leverage to climb the ladders of exposure, influence and power. The catch is this: do unto yourself as you would want others to do unto you. In other words, to be seen and taken as a wielder of power and authority, you have to see yourself as such. You have to take yourself as the best, think and act like it, so much so that every fibre of your being is saturated with YOU (not to the extent of being proud though). Only then can you attract the bees to your sweet scenting flowers.

This brings us to the concept of SELF. The four letter word that wields enough power to grant you that thing that you wish for. This concept is a very critical step especially when taking on the challenge of writing a book and eventually becoming an author of repute.

What is the self? Many would answer by touching their bodies. In a way they could be right in the sense that people first develop a notion of self that is based largely on the physical body. Some others have a notion of self that goes beyond the physical self. These notions include social identity, reputation, and other factors. They think of self as something that exists 'inside'.

Self is a broad term and has many meanings and varying usage.

I would like to define self as the totality of you, including your body, your sense of identity, your reputation (how others know and see you), as well as how you see yourself. Self is both physical and mental.

You shouldn't focus on why you can't do something, which is what most people do. You should focus on why perhaps you can, and be one of the exceptions.

~ Steve Case

Under the broad umbrella of self is several other concepts that weave in and around this large term. Self-concept, self-esteem, identity and self-worth are fruits of this large tree, each with their different meanings but still centred on YOU. Let's take a cursory look at each of these terms to see the differences that exist. Our knowledge of these terms is the first and major step to discovering if the sceptre of authority is actually going to be useful in your hands. As we've earlier highlighted, people will only connect with the YOU that you have seen.

Self Concept/Self-Image

Self-concept is your idea(s) about yourself. It is an individual's beliefs about himself. Self-concept is the way people think about themselves. It is unique, dynamic, and always evolving. This mental image of oneself influences a person's identity, self-esteem, body image, and role in society. Self-concept shapes and defines who we are, the decisions we make, and the relationships we eventually form.

'Who am I?' is the question that self-concept begs to answer. Who am I to myself? As a chiropractor, who am I to my patients? As an author, who am I to my readers? As a husband, who am I to my family? This question begs a great deal of critical thinking and reflection.

A person's self-concept is often defined by self-description such as "I am a chiropractor, a doctor, and an author."

Forming a self-concept is not a walk in the park. It is learning to distinguish between one's own body and the rest of the physical world. As an illustration, as we grow up, we have come to learn that some things are always there while others come and go. The chair in the living room is only there at certain times, but our hands and feet are always there.

In light of your profession as a chiropractor cum author. It is necessary to define the basic components of self-concept. These components play a

The way to get started is to quit talking and begin doing.

~ Walt Disney

major role in scheme if things involving your perception of yourself as well as the public's perception of you. These concepts are reflective processes.

Three basic components of self-concept are the ideal self, the public self and the real self. These three components digested separately but taken as one are the needed foundation to understanding all about building a healthy self-concept, one that eventually bears down on your activities and would go a long way in determining how far you are going to go on the roads you are treading.

The **ideal self** is the person that you would like to be, such as a good, moral and well-respected person. It is how you wish you could be at a future time – the person you envision of being and becoming. Sometimes, this ideal view of how you would like to be conflicts with the **real self** (how you really think about yourself). This indecision can sometimes motivate a client to make changes towards becoming the ideal self. However, the view of the ideal self needs to be realistic and obtainable, or you may be at risk for changes in self-concept. **Public self** is what you think others – your patients and readers alike - think of you and this influences the ideal and real self. Positive self-concept and good mental health results when all three components are compatible and are in tandem with each other.

A positive self-concept is an important part of your happiness and eventual success as a chiropractor-author. Individuals with a positive self-concept have self-confidence and set goals they can achieve. Achieving goals reinforces positive self-concept.

Self-concept is based on information you have collected about your values, life roles, goals, skills, and abilities over time.

"We judge ourselves by what we feel capable of doing, while others judge us by what we have already done" are the words of Henry Longfellow and this quote highlights the need for developing a self-concept that reeks of contagious and relatable confidence.

A person who is quietly confident makes the best leader.

~ Fred Wilson

What constitutes a healthy self-concept?

- The ability to know yourself; ability to assess your innate strengths, weaknesses, talents and potentials and leverage on these qualities to achieve maximum expectations

- The ability to be honest with yourself, being true to who you are and what you hold as your values. The best form of honesty often times is that which is borne from you.

- The ability to take responsibility for your choices and actions. The ability to know and accept the fact that whatever results obtainable (or obtained) are a direct result of the efforts you have put in. In other words, no blame game.

- The ability to love and accept yourself as you are, knowing that there's always room to improve and develop any aspect(s) you choose. It's easy to love another but loving oneself is a higher degree of that term. When you love yourself, it becomes easy for others' love to filter in.

The value of having a healthy self-concept becomes the more evident when you recognize how much it influences your ability to manage your emotional experiences, responses and connections to your patients and readers alike. It also determines how far you are willing to go out of your comfort zone to solve a problem, meet a need or achieve a goal. In the context of this text, how far you are willing to go in achieving the power of authority. Moreover, this influences how you utilize your best resources when confronting challenges and problems.

Developing this kind of healthy self-concept can only be borne out of deliberate planning and concentrated efforts. It starts with acknowledging the intrinsic values you possess as a human being, working tirelessly to

We are really competing against ourselves, we have no control over how other people perform.

~ Pete Cashmore

acquire the needed skills to surmount the hurdles along your way to achieving authority.

In essence, when you possess a healthy self-concept, nothing fazes you. You are confident, poised and assured, all these coming as a consequence of being equipped to handle whatever comes your way.

Summarily, your self-concept as an individual, a chiropractor and author effectively determines what you will do or choose not to do at any given moment in time. This in turn, influences greatly the potential you have and possess to do, be, have and achieve your desired objectives as a respected authority and power broker.

It is worthy to note that there are a number of forces that shape and define your self-concept. Some of these forces are of an internal nature while others are from external sources.

Internal sources include what you think about yourself and/or others, what you pay attention to, how you interpret events and how you reframe your successes and failures. External sources include the environment you find yourself and spend most of your time in, your interactions with others and how other people tend to label you.

Self-Worth and Self Esteem

Under the umbrellas of self-concept lie other terms, all pointing at self. These are self-image, self-worth and self-esteem. They sure are related but they are not the same. These two ride on the back of self-concept (self-image).

Your self-worth is an internal state of being that results from an understanding, loving and acceptance of self. It is a direct measure of how you value and regard yourself in spite of the numerous opinion of others. It's therefore something that really doesn't change when external factors or

Always deliver more than expected.

~ Larry Page

circumstances change. Hence, since self-worth is asserted as steady, it stands to mean that it holds power to radically transform lives – your life.

Having a high level of self-worth means having a favourable opinion or estimate of yourself. It means having unwavering faith in yourself and in the abilities you possess in getting the job done; in getting your patients back to health, in writing a book.

Having a high level of self-worth means feeling worthy and deserving of good things – happiness, health, wealth, success, love and authority! All these obtained irrespective of the obstacles and disappointments faced. It means accepting yourself (inclusive of your flaws, weaknesses and limitations) whole heartedly at all times. It is about recognizing the true value of who you are as a chiropractor and author. Having this high level of self-worth means that you are never tossed to and fro by the winds of people's opinions. It means never allowing outcomes to rock the boats of your confidence.

You alone are the most important factor in how you feel about yourself, about your life, accomplishments, circumstances, limitations as well as successes. Personal power comes when you have transcended these.

It's no doubt that having a high level of self-worth has tremendous value. Yet the question that begs answers is; how does one go about building such important trait? How does one create enough self-worth as a chiropractor and an author to empower daily decisions and actions in ways that will help achieve desired goals and outcomes?

The process is simple but needs consistency. Consistency ensures that you build a self-worth of real value. The process takes time hence, building an enviable self-worth is a long term process.

Don't limit yourself. Many people limit themselves to what they think they can do. You can go as far as your mind lets you. What you believe, remember, you can achieve.

~ Mary Kay Ash

Step 1

This is the self-understanding stage and it involves getting to know yourself at a deeper and more profound level. Imagine for s moment that everything you've known and had suddenly is no more. What if you were all that's left? Eventually, how you feel about yourself after everything has been taken away is essentially the measure of your self-worth. If you have a high level of self-worth, then, having everything taken away will not change who you are as a person. It won't shake your confidence as an individual because external circumstances don't count as measurement parameters.

Who you are and how you see yourself are keys to understanding your true value. Honesty with yourself is one of the hallmarks of self-understanding. Honesty in listing your strengths and weaknesses unbiased.

Step 2

The self-acceptance stage. This involves fully accepting yourself in spite of all yur seeming and obvious flaws, weaknesses ad limitations.

Step 3

Self-love stage. This stage basically has you being able to treat yourself with kindness, tolerance and compassion riding on the back of the fact that you have become more aware of what drives you and what doesn't. One simple method of doing this is positive speaking.

Step 4

The recognition stage. When you have fully accepted yourself, and when you've reached a stage where you practice self-love and self-compassion, that's when nothing else defines you but you! Given this, it is helpful to openly acknowledge that pleasing people is not a priority. Just as other

You don't learn to walk by following rules. You learn by doing and falling over.

~ Richard Branson

people have their own opinions and life, you also have yours to contend with.

Step 5

The responsibility stage involves taking full responsibility for your life, for your circumstances and problems alike. This should be done without leveraging or giving out your personal power. To take responsibility means that you have the personal power to change and influence the events of your life and this is the truest definition of AUTHORITY.

To recap, self-concept is how you see yourself.

Self-esteem on the other hand is how you **feel** about yourself. It is a somewhat personal opinion of yourself and this is shaped by your relationships with others, experiences, and accomplishments in life. It encapsulates the thoughts and feelings that you experience at each moment, these thoughts having a direct impact on your results, behaviour and overall performance.

Self-esteem is primarily hinged on sources outside of yourself that you don't actually control. A healthy self –esteem is necessary for a positive self-concept. This is usually achieved by setting attainable goals and successfully accomplishing such goals. These result in an increased self-confidence and feeling valued. Since self-esteem impacts all aspects of life, it is important to establish a healthy view of oneself.

An author with low self-esteem puts little value on himself and his accomplishments. He feels that he is not good enough and that he is worth less than others. This often leads to feelings if shame. Cascading into negative self-talk and struggles with failure.

Even if you don't have the perfect idea to begin with, you can likely adapt.

Victoria Ransom

Self-Concept: Knowing, Loving and Being True to Yourself

Your self-image comes down to how you see yourself in the *present moment*. Yes, the present moment. This includes the tags you give yourself as it relates to your personality as well as the beliefs you have about how your patients and readers alike perceive you.

However, it is always important to know that your self-image isn't necessarily based on reality – the present, physical world. For instance, a person with an eating disorder may have a self-image that makes them believe that they are obese, when in the reality, they are not. In other words, we can assert that a self-image is only your own perception of yourself and has no real backing in reality.

Self-image includes;

- What you think you look like

- How you see your personality

- What kind of person you think you are

- What you believe others think of you

- How much you like yourself or you think others like you

- The status/power/authority you think you have

Image is to do with perception. How you see yourself is important because your consequent behaviour and thinking is hinged on this. More so, the way you relate to others. As a chiropractor and author, this is important because in order for you to gain the most loyal following of patients, readers and the general public alike, you have to form a perfect image of

197

High expectations are the key to everything.

~ Sam Walton

yourself that these sets of people can relate to and not feel awful. People respond to you either negatively or positively according to the confidence you exude. Your confidence in relationships with people depends on the image you have of yourself

Case Study: Sir Roger Bannister

The great story of Roger Bannister is a very inspirational one. For many years and according to legend, experts said that the human body was not capable of running a mile (1609 meters) in under four minutes. In fact, it was a general opinion that this four minute mile was a 'physical barrier' that no man could break without causing significant damage to his health. They argued that not only was it dangerous, it was impossible.

It was spring, on the 6th of May, 1954, during an athletic meeting between the British AAA and Oxford University, that Roger Bannister ran a mile in 3minutes and 59.4 seconds. He crossed the finish line and as a result, broke through the 'four minute mile' barrier. Bannister's story is one of humans holding themselves back, and what can occur if the shackles on the minds are released.

Let's take a trip back into Bannister's origins and we'll understand why his story is a significant inclusion in the journey to becoming an authority.

Roger wanted to be a doctor, and he proceeded to attend medical school in England. He also had another goal – a runner, a star athlete. But we all know that the study of medicine cannot go simultaneous with any other endeavour. You practically go to school all day, and study all through the night. But through it all, he still nurtured the ambition of becoming a track champion. Every day, he would stab classes and meet up with his college track coach. His medical school as every other, had no track teams talk more a track course. This sneaky mode of trainings only earned him about 40 - 45 minutes of spare time. Each day, he trained these amount of

You just have to pay attention to what people need and what has not been done.

~ Russell Simmons

minutes and he'd return to school. To add, Bannister was never born with a silver spoon.

On the other side of the globe were other athletes who wanted to break the four minute barrier. A John Landy, who was born into affluence, had the best team – physicians, trainers, therapists, physiologists and nutritionists, as well as enough money to cater for his needs. He lived his life in training! There was Wes Santee who was similar to Landy; affluent and having the best hands, and a host of other contenders.

In all, Roger Bannister's name stands top of the list because he won the event and broke the so-called barrier that had kept athletes chained to the narrow confines of doubt and impossibilities. When people make mention of this feat, they say it was more psychological than physiological.

Roger Bannister was knighted twice; once as an athlete and once as a neurologist! Yes, the same Roger Bannister is reported to have authored a book on neurology.

Why was the breaking of this barrier so significant, so significant to be named as one of the greatest athletic achievements? What made this event so significant was the fact that after Roger Bannister broke the barrier, 16 other runners went on to crack the four minute mile. What had really transpired was the fact that the four minute 'physical barrier' had suddenly and fast graduated into becoming a 'psychological barrier'. This had prevented many a runner from attempting and succeeding at it.

In those 40 – 45 minutes of trainings, it can be deduced that Bannister was totally engaged in all he did. Focused on that one thing he came to do – train. And train he did!

What really made Bannister succeed was HIS THINKING. His belief in the fact that nothing was actually impossible if the mind was conditioned to think so. So often the barriers on our way are simply barriers in our minds. Our beliefs and mind sets play a major role in our eventual

You jump off a cliff and you assemble an airplane on the way down.

~ Reid Hoffman

successes or failures. These beliefs expand or limit our worlds. They have a sort of power over us. If we find a way to conquer those high walls in our minds, it then becomes easy to move unhindered.

What are we saying? As a chiropractor cum author that you are, it is very easy to be weighed down by the many obvious obstacles that you might have encountered during the course of producing and making available your masterpiece. The message from Roger Bannister is simple – see your obstacles as creations of your mind. Conquer them in the same place and watch as you soar on relentlessly. Limits should be seen to have one purpose in our lives – to challenge and inspire one to break and go beyond them. These other runners had been held back by their beliefs and mind-sets.

Mental Rehearsal

What does this mean? How does it influence the attainment of authority as an author?

Roger bannister still remains our case study. We have outlined that his winning of that race was more psychological than physiological. We have also outlined the fact that the mind is the battleground where all sort of wars are fought. The ability to conquer in the physical is borne out of the victory in the mind. Bannister, by winning, showed the relationship(s) that existed between mental rehearsal and performance.

The real question is; does mental practice/mental rehearsal enhance performance? Does mental rehearsal guarantee visible results? Before we delve into the crux of the whole matter, let's define the obvious terms.

Mental rehearsal/practice (also known as visualization or imagery) refers to the cognitive rehearsal of a task in the absence of physical movements. As it relates to an athlete, it is when he pictures his movement or skill in his mind. When an athlete prepares for an event by visualizing the steps required to perform the task, he or she is engaging in mental practice. That

Don't be afraid to assert yourself, have confidence in your abilities and don't let the bastards get you down.

~ Michael Bloomberg

is, an athlete who does this is visualizing the sounds, colours, movements and everything that will be present when the actual skill is executed. Mental rehearsals are often termed 'imagined practice'.

For Roger Bannister, mental rehearsal involved him imagining the tracks on which he would eventually run, as well as the probable shouts of the spectators. The colours of the tracks, colours of running shoes and jerseys, sounds of the gun and whistles, practically everything that would be at play on the big day.

As an author, it is often a wise thing to visualize what you expect from your realities. Caring for and treating your patients, writing as well as publishing and marketing your book is something worth visualizing. It helps you bring the bigger picture into focus, eventually opening you up to numerous ideas to tackle seeming obstacles.

There is this general notion of 'writer's block'. This is a situation wherein nothing comes to your head as a writer who is in the process of writing a book or other literature. The gift of mental rehearsals as it relates to writing is that it takes you out of a stressful state of mind and body. It gives you access to an abundant flow of creativity. That story about chiropractic practice that you are trying to put into a book is very important. Finishing it is important. All that comes after is also important.

You experience stress when you perceive threats or opportunities that you fear you cannot handle effectively. Mental rehearsals help you cope with such stress. How? It helps you improve self-confidence, so you can reduce stress and its effects by visualizing yourself successfully dealing with your challenges. Second, relaxation is often a part of mental rehearsal exercises, and of course, relaxation helps reduce stress.

Mental rehearsals improve concentration. This includes before and after scenes, before settling down to treat a patient, before settling down to craft and write a book, as well as after treating your patient, and after writing

Every time you state what you want or believe, you're the first to hear it. It's a message to both you and others about what you think is possible. Don't put a ceiling on yourself.

~ Oprah Winfrey

your book. Mental rehearsals help to maintain current levels of skill and skill execution as a chiropractor cum author.

With mental rehearsals, you can go from scared to confident chiropractor or author. How? Mental rehearsals open you up to the secrets of how your brain and mind works and this is the highest form of self. DOING (treating your patients and/or writing your book) is always preceded by IMAGINING.

Using visualization to become confident in any situation is not rocket science. Some practical how-tos are;

- Visualize the process (of helping your patient, of holding a pen to write a manuscript, of sitting in front of a typewriter or computer to begin writing and so on). See into your thoughts, words and actions.

- Visualize your success. Visualize your book launch. Visualize your press releases and online presence. Visualize your speaking engagements (that your book will get you). Visualize the bestseller status of your book. Visualize the smiles and handshakes from your satisfied and happy patients. In all, visualize the high points of your success and focus on positive emotions. That exhilarating feeling when you have achieved. Let that emotion fuel your fire!

- Repeat your rehearsals. The impact of one rehearsal cannot be compared to the value you obtain from twenty. Confidence levels will break the charts!

In essence, the objectives of mental rehearsals are to improve your physical skills as a chiropractor and as an author through imagining yourself executing those actions.

I made a resolve then that I was going to amount to something if I could. And no hours, nor amount of labor, nor amount of money would deter me from giving the best that there was in me. And I have done that ever since, and I win by it. I know.

~ Harland Sanders

The Mind and Its Inability to Distinguish Fiction From Reality: Using This Fatal Flaw as Leverage to Attaining Relevance

Every day, our brains grapple and struggle with making various decisions. Irrespective of the fact that this same brain is a powerful organ, this same brain is as complicated as it comes. As perfect as the sculpting of the brain is, there is a fatal 'flaw' that has been discovered that if we take advantage of, we can make vast and meaningful improvements to just about any area of our lives – yes, to your life as a chiropractor and/or an author.

That single 'flaw' is this: the human brain is not able to tell the difference between reality and fiction. It does not know whether or not something is actually real. In other words, it can't tell the difference between something you are thinking about and something that is actually happening.

As abstract as this may sound, this 'flaw' is the key to understanding what actually drives the actualization of goals and dreams. The ability to differentiate fiction from reality is the shortest distance between setting and achieving reasonable and SMART goals.

Let's illustrate this to reduce the ambiguity of the statement.

Think about a time, maybe in the past, when you were really frightened. Think of the images that put such fear in you. Tap deeper and feel what you felt at that time, the emotions and all. Think the thoughts you had then too. Amplify these images and exaggerate them to life-like proportions. Keep running this through your mind over and over again.

If you've done this, you'd probably be feeling nervous. Goosebumps and rising hairs. You're a little scared at reliving that experience. Maybe not as scared as you were at that time.

So often people are working hard at the wrong thing. Working on the right thing is probably more important than working hard.

~ Caterina Fake

So, how is it that even though you're sitting comfortably in your living room reading this book and feeling relaxed, safe and secure, that replaying that scary past over gin in your mind rekindles the feelings and worry you had when the actual experience was taking place? The same way goes for an ecstatic feeling. Dwell on it and keep replaying it and you'll find out that those same feelings of then are being replicated in the present where you sit.

The brain can be likened to a computer. The brain's job is to make files based on information that it is fed, usually through our senses of touch, sight, hearing and so on, but sometimes through our thoughts.

See it in this light. If you have a lover, being in the same room will elicit a warm, romantic feeling. However, looking at their picture and thinking about them in their obvious absence will do the same thing and elicit same feelings. Even better is just mere thinking about them, no picture as incentive or motivation. The brain only reacts to the image (or file). It really doesn't care how the image or information is received, by physical presence, by picture reminders or by 'thought'.

All this means is that you have the ability to build your own files, even when the actual real world experience is lacking. Using your imagination, you can alter these files by imagining new information and the brain simply works on it.

All thought is generated from the mind, both conscious and unconscious. Your conscious mind, which is dominant, is the means by which the subconscious receives its information, stores it, and goes on to work to attract, create or bring it into the real, physical world, what you eventually come to know and accept as your truth or reality, resulting in your day to day life experiences.

The subconscious mind makes no determination or judgements concerning the validity or correctness of the data being fed it. It is simply designed to store whatever data is given to it (which can be accessed for later use) by

Trust your instincts.

~ Estee Lauder

the conscious mind. In other words, the conscious mind can analyse and make judgement as to the truth or validity of the information it has processed.

How does this help in your quest to attain that authority? Simple.

Everything about being a chiropractor-author starts and ends with value. Seeing a need or problem and creating value that will solve such a problem. Using this file analogy, it simply translates to picking a target problem for improvement – then design, imagine and create a new set of files to correct it.

Since our brain cannot tell real from imagined experiences, it become easy to feed it with raw data in form of the needs we want to create solutions for. In trying to market your brand as a chiropractor, think of the problems you are going to solve. Create new files to deal with such. Imagine positive scenes in which you solve these problems or make adjustments.

It is all about twisting reality to fit our beliefs. The realities of being a chiropractor and/or author twisted to fit into your belief that these paths are the link to obtaining the power of authority and the influence and exposure that come with them.

If your confidence and self-esteem are low as a chiropractor and author, imagine scenes in which your confidence is increased, imagine being praised for your efforts as a leading expert in the chiropractic practice, being successful as a chiropractor and author, or finally receiving the acceptance/affection from your patients and reader base for your book.

There's lots of bad reasons to start a company. But there's only one good, legitimate reason, and I think you know what it is: it's to change the world.

~ Phil Libin

CONCLUSION

WRITING A BOOK THAT REALLY WORKS

The preceding chapters have highlighted and outlined the basic importance of getting the world to know you and the true value you bring to the marketplace. You have seen what it means to wield some measure of authority as an expert chiropractor who has a book to his credit. Nothing beats such influence. With such influence, you establish yourself as the default expert on matters relating to chiropractic. Furthermore, your reputation grows exponentially, eventually reaching enviable peaks, all these achievable by WRITING A BOOK. Yes, stringing words and sentences together to create meaningful content that will reach a target audience. *Writing a book is akin to putting your experience on paper.*

The biggest question often asked by other wannabe chiropractor-authors is "Where would I find the time to write a book?" "I am swamped daily with patients", "I don't have enough spare hours". On and on they go. One sure way to go is engaging the services of freelance writers who will be able to help you create a book at a fair price. If writing isn't your strength as a chiropractor, do explore this option. It's no shame. Of what use is struggling to write a book when it is obvious that you lack the necessary requisites to doing so?

'How do you get a book written' ranks as a second question. Simple! Start thinking about five to ten main points that you have been able to glean from your journey as a chiropractor. Then think of the most poignant stories and experiences that support these points. They could help create the spark that would eventually be the flame that your budding writing career needs.

If you're not a risk taker, you should get the hell out of business.

~ Ray Kroc

Read! Read! Read!. More and more people neglect this important part about writing. The fact that you would soon become an author should not give you an excuse not to read. It is vital to fill the voids Work with drafts.. First drafts are always horrible. Not to worry, it's the same for everyone. Out of this seeming ugliness is what will eventually become a masterpiece. By reading other authors' book specifically chiropractor-authors' books (if you could lay hands on them), you'll learn what works, what doesn't, absorb new words and vocabularies and above all immerse yourself in the world of writing. *A writer who never reads cannot be an author!*

Writing your own authority book will transform your business riding on the back of the experience you have gathered over the years as a chiropractor and revered expert professional. In this book you have been able to read through and sift nuggets of wisdom on how different business people (chiropractors or not) have used books to acquire more clients, raise fees, and accelerate their sales, ultimately gaining the power of authority.

While writing a book may seem like a very simple step to some chiropractic professionals, some find it a daunting mountain to climb. The reality is, it is the same as any other strategy for growing your business: you need a plan, with steps and deadlines, and you need to follow that plan.

And often the best way to make sure you get through that plan is to work with someone who has done it before. Yes, find someone, a retired or serving chiropractor, who has travelled such writing lane before and make him an ally. You'd be amazed at the wealth of useful information that will be poured out to you - you'll find much ease in charting these unfamiliar waters. It is too easy to make mistakes when you try to do something unfamiliar on your own.

Exploring stuff other than the chiropractic you have been used to is surely going to be a strange and overwhelming experience. Similarly, when it comes to promoting your book or getting it to the people who need to have it, you need strategies, and probably a partner or two to help you implement them.

Theory is splendid but until put into practice, it is valueless.

~ James Cash Penney

The field of chiropractic is one that has to do with marketing and selling yourself as well as your competencies, expertise and professionalism. All these qualities are what patients aim to see to determine if they will eventually give you their backs and spines to work on. Chiropractic like every other business is a competitive arena. Hundreds of you, probably trained in similar environments and plying trades in the same localities, are jostling to amass the best popularity. Once your clients get wind of the fact that you have a book out there, you automatically stand out and are singled out from the crowd as a better expert. One step ahead of your bookless competitors is all you need to hold the scepter of authority. With a book, your book, you don't have to cajole influencers to talk about you. Your book is enough conviction for them to approach you.

Not all books work as well as we have highlighted their importance. Why? Because everyone out there is an author and most of them are not very good! Blunt but true. As a chiropractor and author, if you really want your book to be all that you have envisaged, then you have to work hard at making it better, more engaging, full of value and more authentic than others. For it to command the authority that you seek, *it has to be an extension of you and your expertise as a chiropractor*. Otherwise, it's just another book to litter shelves. Ensuring your book works means that you have to write it well. Mediocre books put people off. They won't communicate your expertise. They'll rather amplify your ignorance and that is bad publicity. Your book has to be good in terms of grammar, construction, content and what have you.

Another way of making your book work well is to design the content to attract ideal clients. As a chiropractor, you know well that what you possess in terms of experience and professionalism matters most. A well written book coming from you, designed to attract ideal clients to your brand allows more than just the ability to add the 'author' tag to your name or bio. You can send a great book into the world confidently knowing that it will represent you, position you, brand you and grow you. Always remember that people will only ache for what appeals to them.

Sustaining a successful business is a hell of a lot of work, and staying hungry is half the battle.

~ Wendy Tan White

Ultimately, your book(s) may or may not be written as benevolence pieces. Owing to the amount of time, resources and brain power that you have put in, in the long run, there will be the question of making profits. You are not being a greedy and money-lusting individual by thinking in such manner. As much as you have put value out there, it is only natural that returns come in to further add spice to the stress. Making money from your book is a function of how well you are able and willing to go the extra mile to generate such income. Your several years as a chiropractor have taught you a thing or two about business and charging premium. Translating this experience into marketing of your book is key to making sure that you get the desired returns from the appreciation of the value(s) you have put out.

There's a saying that nothing good comes easy. The best soups aren't cheap. Leveraging on several factors to make sure you get access to the power of authority is hard work to say the least. You cannot reap from a land where your sweat has never dropped. It is no small feat getting a book out there neither is it child's play in making sure that such book generates the buzz it has been made to. As much as we have said that your book is a sure ticket to exposure, it is actually all about you. Without you, there's no experience, no value and ultimately, no book. The sooner you realize also that nothing comes from nothing, you will be able to sow the necessary seeds which will eventually be your beanstalk to accessing giants.

In all, writing a book by leveraging on your history as a chiropractor is one of the best ways to get the word out there that you exist as one of the foremost authorities. Eventually, the aim of writing a book is not to establish you as ONE OF THE EXPERTS. The ultimate yardstick to measure how much power of authority you have been able to amass is by being addressed as THE EXPERT. As THE EXPERT, you are the only one who really matters; you are always at the top of every potential guru list; your online rankings and ratings are off the charts; you command a presence that is envied the world over. You not only occupy a permanent place in the hearts of those who have become inspired by you – your

Your most unhappy customers are your greatest source of learning.

~ Bill Gates

patients, friends, family, competitors, peers – and when this happens, there's practically no limit to the amount of authority you wield. You have become a creator, revered and worshipped.

Writing a book is a challenge. A worthy attempt at giving the world a piece of you and what you represent. You cannot afford to do it anyhow. Take a deep breath and count the cost. It's cheaper than you think.

YOU are the one that your book seeks to sell.

YOU are the reason why the book is being birthed in the first place.

YOU are the reason the world waits earnestly.

YOU are the only source of your value.

Conscious efforts must be made to present an enviable you to the world, a you that speaks of qualitative input and a contagious personality.

The challenge of crating and writing a book is no small feat. Putting down all your expertise, professionalism and years of experience in words is a Herculean task, not to be undertaken by any who has a faint heart.

Your background as a chiropractor comes to bear in the eventual exposure that you book deserves. It is first about YOU, your brand. Who or what you are. The contents you carry whether mentally, physically or otherwise form the contents of your book. Hence, when your book goes out there, whoever takes readership of it should more or less, read into you – your passion and experience. Only when a reader is able to do this is there going to be an exchange of ideas and passion. You exemplify what they have sought and are still seeking. You become the perfect answer to their numerous questions. They become loyal and diehard fans of you and your work, doing all they can to make sure that the light and insight your book gives never dims. They go further in recommending you to their close circles of friends and family.

Wonder what your customer really wants? Ask. Don't tell.

~ Lisa Stone

But all these are in the future tense. The big question being how does the book get to the readers' shelves and consequently their hands? How do they get to make the choice in choosing your book over a plethora of other similar literature? How do they develop and maintain the loyalty to your brand if in the first instance, they have nothing to base their trusts on?

All these questions are answered by one simple term – marketing. A very often used word that has to do with getting the world aware of you, your brand and the services you offer as a chiropractor and an author.

Without marketing, your brand and your book are in danger of obscurity. Whatever is not made known could as well remain hidden. This is the rule of thumb. Of what use is writing a book if it's going to remain a permanent adornment to your dressing table, blessing none other than yourself? What is the pint of writing a book if at the end of the day poverty still clings to your suits? As much as we would like to downplay it, every author dreams of getting revenue from his book(s). Sweat and stress have to pay off and there is no other means of getting rewards for hard work than through targeted sales of the value you have so lovingly and painstakingly poured out into the world.

Marketing of yourself and your brand is the first major step in getting and inching closer to the authority that you crave, for it opens you up to many possibilities and opportunities which if harnessed, would be the ultimate stepping stone to the seats of influence.

Whatever channel of marketing is employed is aimed at getting maximum returns. Be it traditional means of marketing and advertisement or the more modern media channels, all is aimed at getting the desired exposure, which will eventually translate to a wide readership. Wide readership then cascades into greater demand for you and your value, the ripple effect eventually culminating into a smiling bank account.

Of more importance is the fact that your patients, clients and customers alike will only resonate with a YOU they can trust. A YOU that believes in

If you're passionate about something and you work hard, then I think you will be successful.

~ Pierre Omidyar

himself. A YOU that has a huge load and store of confidence. A YOU that is never ashamed of his strengths and weaknesses, nor is battling with a low opinion of himself and his brand. A YOU that knows how to leverage his best gifts and ideas to fashion the best values.

Your customers want to always see a chiropractor and an author who has mastered his mind so well that the fruits thereof are worth plucking and feeding fat on. Nobody wants to associate himself with a mediocre or mediocrity. Nobody would bother to purchase value from someone who is a loser in his mind as well as in the physical. The mid stands at the canter of any man's core and is the thin line between his efforts and the resulting performance and eventual results. Conquer in your mind and the physical is a win! Leveraging on these attributes is key to obtaining desired dividends of hard work.

Uniqueness is key too. This differentiates you from the rest. It gives you an edge over your peers and competitors in industry, by leveraging on certain qualities that set you apart from others in terms of the value you are adding as well as how well you've been able to package such value.

Summarily, the totality of achieving influence and utmost authority is hinged on several factors that start with YOU as an individual, who has mastered himself and is able to pour himself out in measures that a wide readership would gladly draw from, irrespective of the constraints of price and competition. Once your patients and readers are able to trust the YOU that they have seen in the books, they will have no problem in trusting the YOU they would eventually meet. They would always look forward to more value from you and wouldn't mind going out of their way to make sure you remain on a pedestal higher than others. In other words, whatever authority you seek as an individual is in the hands of your audience. They will only hand it over to you if and only if you have proofed yourself withy in self, character, passion and value.

So my dear fellow chiropractor, there is nowhere your intellect and expert knowledge would be more relevant than in the pages of the book that you

When you find an idea that you just can't stop thinking about, that's probably a good one to pursue.

~ Josh James

know you are called to create. Let the book speak your language but more importantly, let it resonate with the inner whisper that calls you to share the message that you were born to give to this world. Give your patients, their children, your community, your city, and the world that which can inspire them to redefine what is possible for themselves. Go out there and give the world your light and your message!

33140544R00133

Made in the USA
Middletown, DE
12 January 2019